Cracking Creative Writing in KS1

75+ Fun Activities for Key Stage 1 That Will Improve Grammar and Punctuation Too!

David Horner

We hope you and your pupils enjoy using the ideas in this book. Brilliant Publications publishes many other books to help primary school teachers. To find out more details on all of our titles, including those listed below, please go to our website: www.brilliantpublications.co.uk.

Other books written by David Horner
  Cracking Creative Writing in KS2
  Cracking English Grammar in Key Stage 2

Books in the Developing Reading Comprehension Skills series:
  Classic Poetry Years 3-4
  Classic Poetry Years 5-6
  Classic Children's Literature Years 3-4
  Classic Children's Literature Years 5-6
  Contemporary Children's Literature Years 3-4
  Contemporary Children's Literature Years 5-6
  Non-fiction Years 3-4
  Non-fiction Years 5-6

Published by Brilliant Publications Limited
Unit 10
Sparrow Hall Farm
Edlesborough
Dunstable
Bedfordshire
LU6 2ES, UK

www.brilliantpublications.co.uk

The name Brilliant Publications and the logo are registered trademarks.

Written by David Horner
Illustrations by Gaynor Berry

© Brilliant Publications Limited 2022

Printed ISBN: 978-0-85747-965-5
ePDF ISBN: 978-0-85747-973-0
First printed in 2023

The right of David Horner to be identified as the author of this work has been asserted by himself in accordance with sections 77 and 78 of the Copyright, Designs and Patents Act 1988.

All rights reserved. Apart from any use permitted under UK copyright law, no part of this publication may be reproduced or transmitted in any form or by any means, electronic or mechanical, including photocopying and recording, or held within any information storage and retrieval system, without permission in writing from the publishers or under licence from the Copyright Licensing Agency Limited. Further details of such licenses (for reprographic reproduction) may be obtained from the Copyright Licensing Agency Limited, 5th Floor, Shackleton House, 4 Battle Bridge Lane, London SE1 2HX (https://cla.co.uk)

Contents

Title	SPaG	Cross-curricular links	Page
Year 1			
Always on the Go	Conjunction 'and'	Parts of the body	9
4 x 4 x 4 x 4	Conjunction 'and'	Seasons	11
Body Language	Verbs with '-ing'	Parts of the body	13
How Noisy is the World!	Verbs; vocabulary development	Geography	15
Counting Songs	Numbers as words; plural with '-s'/'-es'	Numbers	17
Goodies and Baddies	Story planning; capital letters for names		19
Shape Shifting	Capital letters and full stops for sentences	Geometric shapes	21
The Five Senses of –	Adding suffix '-s' to verbs	Senses; Christmas	23
One and Two	Vocabulary; sentence development		25
Nice and … Unnice	Prefix 'un-'; antonyms		27
The Science of Spells	Adjectives	Materials	28
Things – and More Things	Adjectives; group ideas for description and specification		31
Heads and Tails	Writing descriptions	Wild animals	34
Meet the Weather	Capitals for names and pronoun 'I'	Weather	37
Rhyming Riddles	Rhymes; first person pronoun 'I'; sentence building; syllables		39
Time Travel	Capital for pronoun 'I'	Time	41
Can I Just Ask You …?	Writing questions; question marks		43
Would You Rather …?	Question marks; conjunction 'or'		45
That's Not My Question!	Question marks; full stops; asking questions; capital letters		47
Too!	Exclamation marks; capital for pronoun 'I'		49
A Mouse's Tale	Rhymes; nonsense words; exclamation marks	Time	51
Daze of the Week	Spelling days of the week; acrostic		53
Rhyme Time	Question marks; using speech to tell a story; sequencing a text; rhyme		55
Guided Fantasy	Sequencing sentences to form a narrative		57
That Does It!	Spelling patterns		59
Let's Write a Musical		Music	61

Contents

Title	SPaG	Cross-curricular links	Page
Opposites Attract	*Synonyms; antonyms; conjunctions 'and' and 'but'; using a thesaurus*		62
Simply Similes	*Similes; synonyms; using a thesaurus*		64
Year 2			
Just Because	*Using 'because' for subordination*		66
Once Upon a Time	*Past and present tense verbs; compound sentences using 'but'*		68
Special Senses	*Coordination using 'but'; compound sentences; synonyms*	Senses	70
There's Always a But	*Compound sentences; conjunction 'but'*	Materials	72
Sometimes	*Separating words*		73
Countdown to …	*Instructions; commands; drafting; sequencing*		75
Then and Now	*Verb forms – present and past progressive; sequencing*		77
Let's Go Ladder-ing	*Progressive verb form '-ing'; planning writing; drafting writing*		79
Poems for Presents	*Present progressive verb form '-ing'; exclamation marks*		81
Body Beautiful	*Nouns; adjectives; noun phrases; commas in lists; suffixes*		83
What's My Word?	*Capital letters; adverbs for sequencing; commands; alphabetical order*		84
Father William's Diary	*Past and present tenses; days of the week, capital for pronoun 'I'*		85
The Museum of Me	*Present and past tenses; autobiographic writing*		88
When …	*Days of the week; months of the year*	Festivals; weather; seasons	90
The Twelve Months	*Months of the year; the suffix '-y'*		92
What Are Heavy?	*Adjectives; alphabetical order; nouns, expanded noun phrases*		93
Making Magic	*Rhyme; adjectives; adverbs; commands; exclamation marks; chronological ordering*		95
Full Colour	*Expanded noun phrases; exclamation marks; question marks*		97

Contents

Title	SPaG	Cross-curricular links	Page
As I Was Going to …	Subordination using 'that'; past progressive tense; question marks; riddles		99
Something to Shout About!	Interjections; exclamations; exclamation marks		101
A Few of My Favourite Things	Commas in lists; expanded noun phrases; plural noun suffixes; subordination		102
All Creatures Great and Small	Full stops; question marks	Animal habitats; food chains; RE	104
This Hand	Commas in lists; handwriting; descriptions and specifications; adding '-s' to verbs		105
On Your Marks!	Punctuation as art: full stops, commas, question marks, exclamation marks		107
Chain Whispers	Question marks; exclamation marks; speech marks		109
Oh, Do Be So Silly!	Apostrophes for contraction		110
I am a Who – Not a What	Adjectives; nouns; apostrophes for contraction		112
Simply Super!	Prefix 'super-' for adjectives; apostrophes for contraction		113
Two Little Words	Compound sentences; apostrophes for contraction		115
The Caretaker's Crocodile	Alphabetical order; apostrophes for single ownership; possessive adjectives; conjunction 'and'		117
A First Abecedarius	Capital letters; alphabetical order; tense consistency; dictionary use		119
The Animals Do Fancy Dress	Apostrophes for single ownership		121
Adventures with Adverbs	Changing adjectives to adverbs		123
Silly Suffixes	Suffixes		125
Three of a Kind	Adding suffixes '-er' and '-est' to adjectives		127
Haiku for Beginners	Adjectives in comparative and superlative forms; haiku		129
Happy Endings	Suffixes; spelling patterns; riddles		131
Two's Company	Compound nouns; riddles		133

Contents

Title	SPaG	Cross-curricular links	Page
Spot the Difference	*Silent letters; riddles*		135
Shape Riddles	*Technical vocabulary; riddles*	Geometric shapes	136
Writing Recipes	*Plural '-s' suffix*	Numbers; fractions	137
Who am I?	*Sequencing; writing draft; speech marks; question marks; riddles*		139
Now We Are Six	*Subordination; tense consistency; capital for pronoun 'I'; conjunction 'but'*		141
Welcome to Word World!	*Word classes; alliteration; terminology*	Measurement of weight and volume; money	143
Crazy Creatures	*Similes; pronouns*		144
All Things Bright and Beautiful	*Expanded noun phrases; similes*	Flowers	146
To Boldly Go	*Simple and compound sentences; capitals for names; anagrams*		148
The Incredible It	*Similes; compound sentences; synonyms; antonyms*		150
The Magic of Metaphors	*Metaphors*		152
Digging Into Dictionaries	*Nouns; verbs, adjectives; adverbs; progressive verb form*		154

Acknowledgements	156
References	157

Introduction

Moods and Tenses
bother my senses.
Adverbs, Pronouns
make me roar.
Irregular verbs
my sleep disturb –
They are a regular bore.

As hard as I've tried, I can't find any background information on that unhappy little rhyme – no authorship, no date of composition, no place of origin. Nothing. It's been with me for many years now, so it must be pretty old; and written, we must assume, by one of the all time greats – Anon.

My first book for Brilliant Publications, *Cracking Creative Writing in KS2*, was aimed at Key Stage 2 children and is a collection of writing activities. My second book, *Cracking English Grammar in Key Stage 2*, faced the SPaG monster head on and I carefully designed activities centred around the KS2 English Curriculum.

This third book, *Cracking Creative Writing in KS1*, combines the two, offering over 75 different writing suggestions that I have found work, with great success, with 5-7 year olds. I have highlighted where the writing activities can be used to teach and reinforce the grammar, spelling and punctuation elements covered in the Key Stage 1 National Curriculum.

As a one or two day visitor to a school, I would rarely have more than an hour with any one class – and, sometimes, this hour included my introductory reading. So, when it came to the writing activity, the need was always for immediacy and clarity. I've tried to explain each activity as straightforwardly as possible, so that the children can engage as young writers and appreciate the power of the English language. I have always wanted to make writing enjoyable and boost children's literary confidence.

The programmes of study for English state, uncompromisingly, that an 'explicit knowledge of grammar … gives us more conscious control and in our language'. Throughout, their emphasis is on analysis and the learning of rules. There is a fear that committed teachers will spend more time 'explicitly' teaching the rules rather than allowing time for focused writing.

For Years 1 and 2 the focus is inevitably weighed in favour of how children shall write (transcription), rather than what they might write (composition). To me composition comes first. I want every young writer, in every classroom, to have something of their own at the end of their writing session. I want children to engage with their prescribed element of English through the activities in this book: to manipulate and play with it and discover themselves what can be done. I have considered the vast differences in writing competencies and confidence in any Key Stage 1 class, and have therefore included many suggestions for differentiation.

Introduction

In those classroom sessions, small errors were inevitable in so many first drafts. Therefore, in presenting examples of children's work here, I have taken the liberty of tidying up their spelling and punctuation to what, in 1989, Professor Brian Cox (no, not that one) called, quite simply, the 'secretarial aspects' of writing. I must, however, confess that I was particularly sad to lose valiant and ambitious efforts such as 'tepecher' and 'stecytofypodee'' all the same.

Most of the examples of children's writing appear on separate pages to make it easier to display them to classes using a visualiser or to photocopy the page to hand out to students.

In my earlier books, the examples of children's writing came directly from classrooms. This time, because of the Covid 19 restrictions, these have been supplemented with items provided by the children and grandchildren of friends and family, who agreed to join in. I am very grateful for all of their trialling and testing along the way.

Finally, I'm left wondering what our despondent, opening rhyme-writer would make of it all, a hundred, possibly two hundred years later. Anon would almost certainly fit right in to English in the current Key Stage 1 classroom; and then hopefully have some creative, and worthwhile, fun trying out the ideas here – as I hope you and your young writers will go on to do too.

Always on the Go

My feet kick and stamp.
My legs run and dance.
My hands wave and tickle.
My arms hold and hug.
My mouth eats and talks.
My elbows bend and poke.
My neck turns and twists.
And my bottom never sits still.

Shauna

Always on the Go

What to do

* Shauna has to be typical of 6- and 7-year olds, enjoying her non-stop self and also the chance to reflect on and describe how different parts of her body work.

* Start the activity by making a collection together of the main parts of the human body. The notes and guidance to the science curriculum has a list of a dozen or so, that you might draw on.

* In their poem, children are going to write a single line/sentence for any or all of these parts, focussing on the particular things each part does.

* The pattern of each line is as in Shauna's example. For each line, writers have to think of two things each body part does.

* Challenge pupils to think of two different activities for each part – expressed in two different **verbs**, linked by the **conjunction** *and*.

* For a closing line, writers can have a choice of starting either '*And my bottom …*' or '*And my brain …*' and write just a single thing that they believe fits their chosen part.

Differentiation suggestion

* More able children could be challenged not to repeat any verb in the whole poem.

4 x 4 x 4 x 4

Summer

We go on holiday
and eat ice creams
and the sun shines
and the bees buzz.

Autumn

Leaves go all gold
and it gets colder
and it's harvest festival
and night comes more.

Nola and Evie (extract)

4 x 4 x 4 x 4

What to do

* Here's a writing idea directly linked to the study of seasons in science. There are four seasons, so that's the first '4' of the title ticked off.

* Begin by putting up each of the seasons as headings and ask the children to suggest features they know of each one. You could suggest the following topics to stimulate ideas:

  - animals – ones they will notice and how they behave
  - the weather
  - plants, flowers and trees
  - length of day and night
  - games to play
  - clothes to wear
  - food and drink
  - cultural and religious festivals.

* Explain to the children that they are going to celebrate the seasons in a poem. They will write things about each season, so their poems will have four verses.

* Each verse has to include four details related to that season to give each verse four lines. It's important to encourage children to include different aspects of each season in each verse's four lines.

* Each line (and clause) can be linked with the **conjunction** *and* to make each season feel of a piece. It also makes each verse a single **sentence**, needing one **capital letter** and one **full stop**.

Differentiation suggestion

* The final '4' is entirely optional. Challenge more able writers to use just four words in each line to describe each seasonal feature they choose.

Body Language

We are
> jumping, singing, walking,
>> eating, sleeping, listening,
>>> reading, writing, painting,
>>>> laughing, playing, swimming,
>>>>> breathing, growing, running,
>>>>>> messing, skipping, dancing
>>>>>>> girls!

Naomi, Maya, Niamh

Body Language

What to do

* That's one way for children to write a single **sentence** containing (possibly) the longest **noun phrase** ever!

* More importantly, it's a good way for them to see and reflect on the ever-increasing range of things they and their bodies need, and are able, to do.

* Start by collecting together a board-full of things the children do every day. You'll very quickly get a large number of **verbs** – literally doing words.

* Tell the children that they are going to write pieces to celebrate their bodies by using any of the verbs you've collected plus any more they think of as they write.

* Divide the children into small groups, with each group working on a single piece of writing. The aim is to think and write fast – you might even set a time limit for the activity.

* Explain that in their writing, they will need to change each verb they write down into its **progressive form** by adding the **suffix** *-ing*. This changes the root verbs into **adjectives**, all leading to and describing the final **noun** – *girls* in the example above – with groups choosing a concluding noun, depending on the mix.

* They should start their writing, as the three girls did in their poem with *We are* and then write down as many words as they can in the time you allow.

* Once groups have their collection of activities, they now need to check if any further spelling changes are needed, for example, changing '*write*' to '*writing*' or '*skip*' to '*skipping*'. Groups can also now put **commas** between the adjectives to separate them and make the whole easier to read.

* These make great pieces to read aloud and perform. They can also be linked to work in science on our bodies and our need for exercise, diet, mental activity, etc.

How Noisy is the World!

Rain in Summer

How beautiful is the rain!
How it clatters along the roofs
Like the tramp of hoofs,
How it gushes and struggles out
From the throat of the overflowing spout!
Across the window-pane
It pours and pours;
And swift and wide,
With a muddy tide,
Like a river down the gutter roars
The rain, the welcome rain!

                            Henry Wadsworth Longfellow (extract)

How noisy is the world!

How loud is all the traffic!
How the lorries and the buses roar like wild bears!
The cars race. The vans rush everywhere.
Brakes squeak and horns hoot.
At the lights it crawls and creeps and stops.
    The traffic, the dirty traffic!

                            Jibreel and Yasin

How Noisy is the World!

What to do

* Longfellow was a nineteenth century New England poet and one of very few Americans to be celebrated in Poet's Corner in Westminster Abbey.

* The lines from 'Rain in Summer' come from near the start of a much longer poem. They squeeze in a number of strong **verbs** describing the noise and the movement of the downpour: *clatters, roars, gushes, struggles, pours*. Focus on these when you look at the extract, picking them out and discussing their meanings.

* Verbs aren't called 'doing words' for no reason; and here they keep the writing, as well as all the water, moving powerfully along.

* There are lots of other scenes which have both movement and noise. For example:

    the seaside   a funfair   playtime   a storm

    the jungle   a sports event   a party

* Let children choose a scene to describe or give them one of the above. Ask them first to write down all that is happening – including as many verbs as they can, to describe the sounds and action.

Differentiation suggestion

* It's even better, particularly for less confident writers, if children can go on a 'listening walk', collecting material as they go. That is what Jibreel and Yasin did. Back in the classroom, they looked again at the extract from 'Rain in Summer' and used it to shape their notes into their poem, using some of Longfellow's sentence openings, his use of similes and his closing line – with that interesting change of adjective!

Counting Songs

One gold goldfish and

two long rulers and

three pointy pencils and

four red chairs and

five colourful crayons and

six super storybooks.

Luke

Counting Songs

What to do

* Start this activity by asking children to write down a short list of different things they can see around them. Challenge them to write down only things beginning with different letters or letter sounds. Encourage children to find at least six words, as Luke did in the example, but more able pupils might be able to find more.

* On a fresh page ask children to start their counting song by writing the numbers one to six as words down the page. Next they should write down their six chosen things (**nouns**) in any order, leaving a gap prior to the noun.

* In the gap before each noun they should add an **adjective** to describe the noun to make it more interesting.

* Next, children should add the connective *and* at every line-end to join it all together.

* Finally, remind them check there is a **capital letter** at the start, a **full stop** at the end and that every noun after the first one needs to be plural, so they will need to add *-s* or *-es*.

Differentiation suggestions

* Instead of asking children to choose things they can see around them, you could give them a topic, such as:

animals	toys	transport	weather
clothes	sports kit	people who help us	

* More confident writers, possibly approaching Year 2, can practise using **commas** for separation instead of the connective *and*. You could also challenge them to use more than one adjective in any one line.

Goodies and Baddies

Goodies and Baddies

Spider Cabbage. He is a nasty wizard. He lives in a dark cave.

Apple Crumble Sunshine. She is good and clever. She can do magic too.

Grey Winter. This is a big dog. He helps the wizard do very bad things.

Hamster Seaside. He is Apple Crumble's best friend. He likes playing tricks all the time.

In our story Spider makes trees disappear. Apple Crumble and Hamster trick him and get the trees back.

Jess and Lily-Ann

Goodies and Baddies

What to do

* Fairy stories and science fiction might be separated by the years, but their characters are almost interchangeable: you get goodies (Little Red Riding Hood, Princess Leia) and you get baddies (Captain Hook, The Daleks) and very little in between.

* Sometimes, works of fiction signal their characters' natures through their names: Charles Dickens' Ebenezer Scrooge, Roald Dahl's Verruca Salt. Maybe the best examples are the two aunts in Russell Hoban's tales of Jack and Captain Najork: Bundlejoy Cosysweet and Fidget Wonkham-Strong.

* In this activity pupils create some brand-new names for story characters.

* Have the children fold a sheet of paper in half. Tell them they are going to make two lists: some likes and some dislikes. They must write their likes on one side of their paper and their dislikes on the other. They should write one like and one dislike only, for each topic. Here are some possible 'like' and 'dislike' topics:

    food   weather   animal   touch   place   colour   season   sound

* When both lists have between six and eight items, writers now draw lines connecting two items on each side of their sheet to make pairs of words. They must not connect words in different halves of their page.

* These pairs of words now become first and last names for story characters. Writers can choose the order of the two words to form the character they want, taking care not to forget to use **capital letters** now those words are names.

* Some or all of these names can now be used in stories. Children can set to work on their stories straight away, or, like Jess and Lily-Ann, begin by writing some sentences to describe each of their characters and give an outline of their story's plot.

Differentiation suggestion

* Less confident writers can sometimes be bursting with ideas! Telling these ideas to an adult – or even older child – who then acts as scribe, can be highly rewarding and liberating for them.

Shape Shifting

Shape Shifting

I am a circle.
I am the sun.
Every day I rise up in the sky.

I am a triangle.
I am a slice of cake
in the kitchen. Eat me.

I am a square.
I am a slice of toast.
I make soldiers for my boiled egg.

I am a rectangle.
I am a book
of interesting pages to read in bed.

Adam

Shape Shifting

What to do

* By the end of Key Stage 1 children are expected to be able to recognise a number of 2D and 3D geometric shapes. Here's an activity that puts mathematics and English together.

* The National Curriculum lists seven shapes in all. Start by writing up all the ones you expect your children currently to recognise.

* Ask them next to suggest objects that are actually one of those shapes and build up group or class collections.

* Explain that they are going to write poems to feature these shapes – and in their writing they are going to become those shapes.

* As Adam's poem on page 21 shows, each small verse is made of three lines:

    + In line 1 writers say which shape they have become.

    + In line 2 they say which real world object they are – one from the collected list or one they have thought of themselves

    + In line 3 they add a detail or two about their object to bring it to life for the reader.

* Remind pupils to check their punctuation. The first line will be a **sentence**, so it should start with with a **capital letter** and end with a **full stop**. The second and third lines could be separate sentences, as in the case of the third verse on page 21, or it could be one continuous sentence as in the second and fourth verses. Point out that the third line only needs to start with a capital letter if it is a brand-new sentence.

The Five Senses of –

Christmas

Christmas smells like pudding.
Christmas sounds like ho ho ho.
Christmas feels like chocolate.
Christmas tastes of cake.
Christmas looks like snow.
　　　Kids it's Christmas.

Tony

The Five Senses of –

What to do

* In this activity children will write a five-line poem to celebrate both a chosen subject and the ways our senses experience its elements.

* Tony's subject was Christmas, but it could be any festival or cultural occasion. It could be one of the seasons; the seaside; playtime; a park; a library; the school dinner hall – in short anywhere or any time when our senses are engaged and exercised.

* A good way to initiate the activity is to ask children to close their eyes and, given a subject, offer sounds, tastes and so on that they think of in relation to it.

* You can provide a list of the key **verbs** for each of the senses, pointing out that in their writing, children will need to add the **suffix** -s to each root word.

* All five lines of the poem start by naming the subject, in Tony's case, Christmas. What the writers have to do now is be sure to choose a different item to put into each of the five lines, so as to ensure variety and completeness of the word-picture.

* Tony felt his poem needed that final flourish and you can suggest the same to your writers, if the idea appeals. Such a closing line can become a refrain for a group or class performance of individual poems.

Differentiation suggestion

* Tony chose to use just one item for each sense, and it feels perfectly complete. However, if more confident writers want to include more items for each sense, that's fine too, so long as there is no repetition.

One and Two

One and Two

One hand can
> write a poem.

Two hands can
> clap ten times really loud.

One foot can
> hop on Friday.

Two feet can
> walk to London and back.

One of us can
> dig under ground and make a huge hole.

Two of us can
> play mums and dads.

Charlotte

One and Two

What to do

✳ Start by writing the title of this poem, 'One and Two', on the board for all the writers to see.

✳ To make this activity work, it is important you introduce the poem one line at a time to the writers. So: *One hand can ...*

✳ This approach allows for pauses in the writing and discussion of the possibilities each opening offers; it also lets writers read their lines out loud, hear what they have written and feel the poem growing.

✳ It also allows the teacher a chance to press the writers for some good, imaginative detail in each line. So, no stopping at the **verb**! Encourage as wide a range of line continuations as possible – from the simply true to the wildly extravagant – offering ideas yourself to indicate what is possible, and the need to be adventurous in ideas and word choice.

✳ When you have exhausted the possibilities for a line, and the children have written their own line, you can then invite them to predict how the next line might begin.

✳ Acknowledge correct guesses, of course, but also make a mental note of any of the 'wrong' suggestions – they can always provide you with material for poetry writing sessions in the future.

Differentiation suggestion

✳ Less confident writers will often stop at the main verb, and if so, ask follow-up questions to elicit further details – for example, How far can you walk? Who do you like to walk with? – for the writer to add the necessary detail.

Nice and ... Unnice

What to do

* It seems there are well over 9,000 English words beginning with the **prefix** un-. If we discount ones like '*uniform*' and '*underwater*' and we save '*unclimbableness*' for another day, it still leaves a lot of words beginning with those two letters.

* It also makes those letters a great means of introducing prefixes to young children. Prefixes work as a quick and clever way of changing the meanings of existing words; most helpfully in the case of *un-*, it changes any word to its opposite meaning.

* Here then is an activity meant to make two posters: one with just root words and one with the prefix *un-* added to each root word.

* Start by asking the children for ways in which we all behave properly and nicely to each other in the classroom. Collect and list their offerings, perhaps *friendly, caring, quiet,* and so on.

* List all their ideas again and now add *un-* to each one so they can clearly see how the prefix works to create the opposite meanings.

* Make the two contrasting posters, one headed *Nice is ...* and the other headed *Unnice is ...* for prominent classroom display. Mission statement and SPaG item done in one.

* Perhaps you're saying the word '*unnice*' doesn't exist? Roald Dahl's *BFG*, that unique word-maker, would give a word new prefixes for dramatic effect, as in *um-possible*. He would even on occasion add a prefix to a word of his own devising – *unjumbly*, for example.

* The BFG calls his habit of playing with and inventing new words '*gobblefunking*'. So, if the children come up with novelties such as '*unbusy*' or '*unconcentrating*', you know what to call it.

The Science of Spells

A spell to make snow that makes snowballs by itself, ready for throwing:

Read, because I now shall tell
what you need to make this spell.

    A window made of hard wood
    A drink made of old cardboard
    A spoon made of red wool
    A tree made of hard plastic
    A book made of sparkly glass
    A cup made of writing paper
    A jumper made of shiny metal
    A brick made of hot water

When you have these things, just say
Abracadabra – right away!

Aaron and Jakob

The Science of Spells

What to do

✳ In science at Key Stage 1 children are expected to look at a range of different materials and the different things that we make with them.

✳ In this activity, children start by showing that they can distinguish between natural materials and made objects.

✳ This might be a good activity for working pairs or small groups; they need a printed copy of the table on page 30. Into each left-hand box they write any one object that can be made using the material named in the box on the right.

✳ Tell the children they are now to see themselves as magicians, able to make magic spells. To make a brand-new spell, they must first cut their completed table into 16 separate pieces and rearrange it so that there are no correct matches between any of the materials and the made objects. These new combinations will be the ingredients for their spell.

✳ The spell-writers now choose what they want this new spell to be able to do and write this as a title on a fresh page.

✳ They now write their list of magical ingredients, preserving the sequence of objects and materials just made. As they write – and to prevent this being merely a copying exercise – they should add at least one **adjective** before each material/**noun**.

✳ Aaron and Jakob were given the rhymes that frame their spell. You can use them too – or make up your own to prove yourself the magician-in-chief.

The Science of Spells

A	made of glass
A	made of wood
A	made of paper
A	made of water
A	made of cardboard
A	made of wool
A	made of plastic
A	made of metal

Things – and More Things

Things with Legs

Next door's dog Harvey
The table where I eat my tea
A spider making a web
The chair I sit on to do my work
Mr Neal when he does PE with us
The blackbird granny feeds in her garden
Me when I run home from school for my snack

Matthew

Things – and More Things

What to do

✳ Matthew's list-poem describes the things he thought of that have legs.

✳ The world holds lots of things and must often seem a pretty chaotic place to children. Here's an activity that starts like a game and develops to get young writers thinking of things organised into particular sets or categories.

✳ For the game you'll need to have made at least one die – more if different groups are trying the activity at the same time. You can either use a cut-out web (see page 33) or cover a cube-shape empty tissue box. On the faces of each die, write six different ideas for a set. Matthew's die had these:

- ◆ Things with Wheels, Things with Wings, Things with Legs, Things with Tails, Things with Numbers, Things with Letters

✳ Each writer rolls the die in turn to find their set-subject. Matthew's throw gave him 'Things with Legs'. At first, children just think of and jot down all the things they can think of that fit their subject. Once they have their list, they write their title, possibly on a fresh page.

✳ Below the title, writers make their collections into list-poems by taking each item in turn and making it into a line of the poem by using whatever extra descriptive words you want to suggest.

✳ Here, finally, are some more ideas for die faces:

- ◆ Soft Things, Hard Things, Small Things, Big Things, Sharp Things, Smooth Things

- ◆ Things that Grow, Noisy Things, Things that Swim, Things that Fly, Things that Open, Things that Shine

Differentiation suggestion

✳ For less confident writers, you might suggest that they add just a single **adjective** before each **noun** from their collection; more independent children need to be encouraged to add several words to make **expanded** (and interesting) **noun phrases** for 'description and specification' – to use the language of the National Curriculum Orders.

Things – and More Things

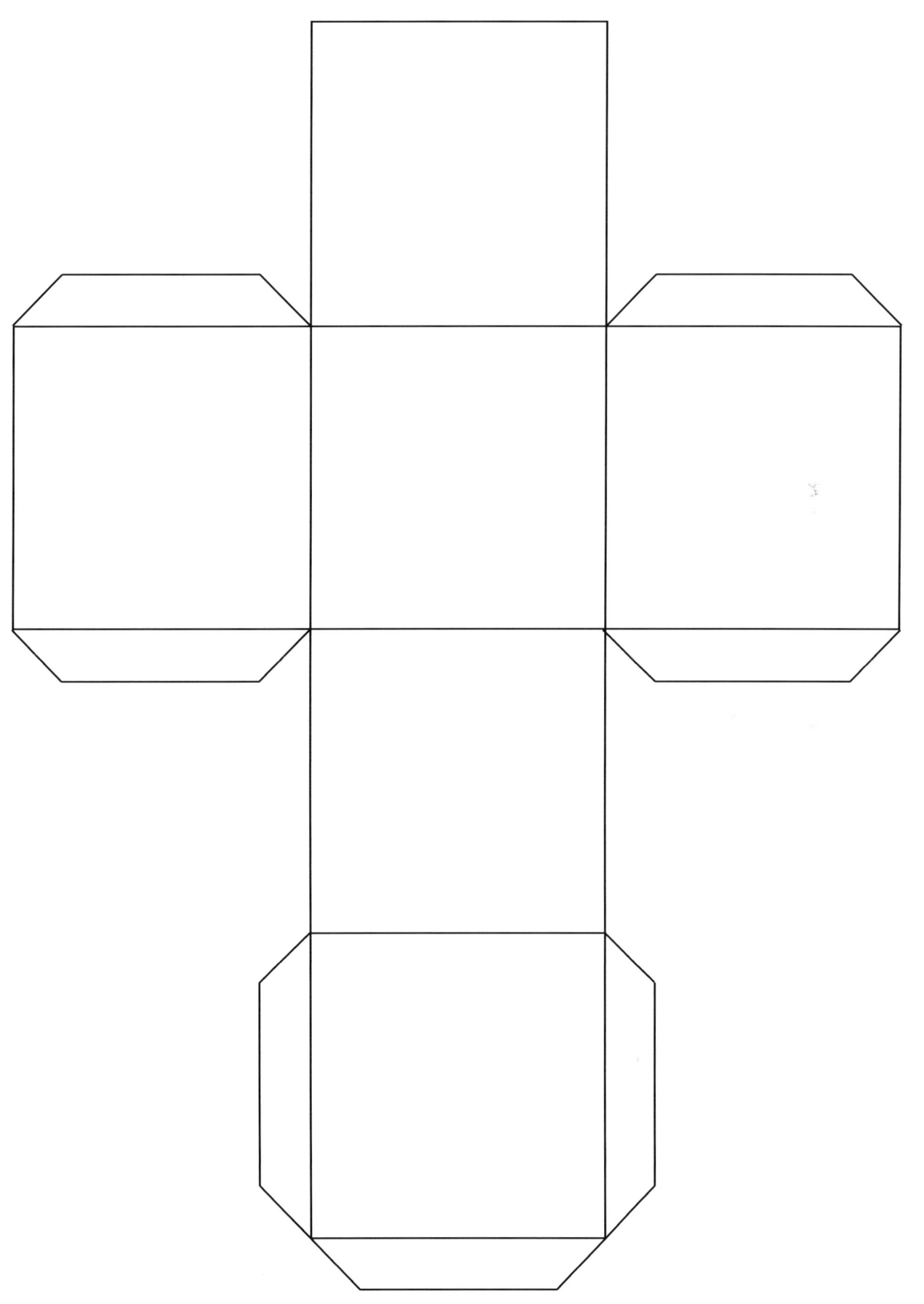

Heads and Tails

The Butterphant

It is half elephant and half butterfly. It is very tall and very heavy. It has a long trunk and huge ears. It is grey all over but the ears have lots of colours on them. It flaps its ears so it can fly. It eats grass and bits of trees. It lives in Africa and comes to your garden in summer.

Connor

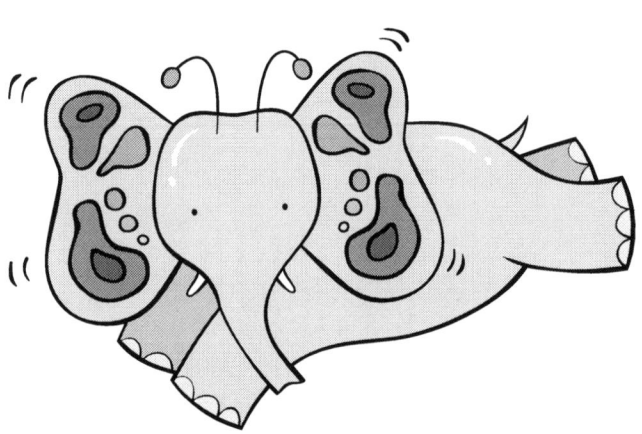

The Jellybird

Half of the animal is a jellyfish and half is a blackbird. It is really squashy and wobbly and has lots of black feathers. It lives in the sea but it can fly up into the air. It builds a nest in a tree for its eggs. It sings a lot and it can sting you too.

Samira

Heads and Tails

What to do

* Well, nature is full of surprises and here are some more! The starting point of the activity is good for group work, so begin by printing one copy of page 36 for each group. Cut up the pages into 24 pieces and give each group a complete set – face down.

* Tell the groups they have 24 cards. Each card is the first or last part of an animal and so now they must turn over the cards to make the 12 different animals by putting two cards together correctly each time.

* Once groups are ready, talk together about the animals, what they know and don't know about them – their appearance, behaviour, diet, habitat.

* Explain now that they should see themselves as explorers and naturalists – future David Attenboroughs. As such, they are now going to discover some never-before-seen creatures by putting cards together in as unlikely ways as possible.

* Tell the children they can only pair up cards that properly join two halves together, with a 'head' and a 'tail' each time. They should play and experiment with combinations until they find ones that most appeal.

* Before any writing, children might usefully make drawings of their new hybrid creatures.

* Children are now going to write descriptions of their creatures to go with their drawings. First, they write the name of their new creature. Next, they write a sentence saying what each half of the animal is made of. Finally, they write their description with the jumble of facts as wondrous and fanciful a combination as possible.

Differentiation suggestion

* Hesitant writers can be helped by being asked to write the creature's name and what makes its two parts. Then, as in the examples by Connor and Samira, they write a sentence for each of the given key aspects: what does their new creature look like? What does it do? What does it eat? Where does it live? Independent writers can write where their imaginations lead them!

Heads and Tails

croco	dile	hedge	hog
ele	phant	hippo	potamus
kanga	roo	octo	pus
jelly	fish	chim	panzee
pen	guin	butter	fly
black	bird	gi	raffe

Meet the Weather

I am Rain.
I make slugs come out to play.
I do a little dance on your lawn.

I am Wind.
I tell the white horses to gallop and jump.
The Pennines block my way like soldiers around Buckingham Palace.

I am Fog.
I make a person look like a ghost.
I do a vanishing trick on the world.

I am Thunder and I am Lightning.
We like to be in a rage.
Even the boldest animals are scared of us.

                          Jodie

Meet the Weather

What to do

* Children are quite used to talking and writing about the weather. The twist in this activity is that, as writers, they will become the weather. This helps the writers to understand the different forms of the weather as active, living forces.

* Start by asking the children for all the different kinds of weather they know. Build up a list for all to see.

* Explain that in their writing, they are now going to imagine they are some of those different types of weather.

* In each verse of a poem they will first introduce themselves by saying which type of weather they are. Each weather they choose will become their new name and as such will need a **capital letter**, as in Jodie's *I am Rain, I am Wind*, etc. This introduction makes line 1 of each verse.

* Below that, each weather must now say something it does when it's at work. Encourage pupils to make their lines interesting and exciting. The forms of the weather are living forces, so the writer's task is to create lines that are equally alive and energetic.

Differentiation suggestion

* More able writers should write (at least) two things, each on a fresh line. In each line, the weather should describe the different things it does. For less able writers, one line is fine, the emphasis being on the need for their line to bring the weather vividly to life.

Rhyming Riddles

I have five letters.
I rhyme with well.
You can find me on the beach.
I am a s _ _ _ _.

Samira

I have nine letters.
I rhyme with smile.
I have a long body and a very big mouth.
I am a c _ _ _ _ _ _ _ _.

Joss

shell; crocodile

Rhyming Riddles

What to do

* As you can see, these riddles have a straightforward four-line structure:

  * Line 1 tells the reader the number of letters in the word to be guessed;
  * Line 2 offers a rhyme for the item to be guessed;
  * Line 3 gives one or two details of this item;
  * Line 4 has just the first letter of the answer.

* Having the whole class create riddles on an agreed theme works well – animals, toys, classroom things, and so on.

* There are lots of rhyming dictionaries available now – for all ages. These can be really useful, helping riddlers find just the right word for Line 2.

* Writers should put the answer to each of their riddles (upside down) at the bottom of their page.

* It's always good to have writers properly road-test their work. You could send riddles off to another class of children; or your writers might visit younger children to read, to try their riddles out in person.

Differentiation suggestions

* Less able writers will probably stick to the safety of one **syllable** words.

* A good approach for more able children is to ask them to make riddles, first with a one syllable word and then words with increasing numbers of syllables in the answer – as in Joss's example above.

Time Travel

In one second I can blink my eyes.

In one minute I can run upstairs.

In one hour I can go to the park and back.

In one day I can fly to Florida.

In one week I can read a chapter book with dad.

In one month I can knock down a wall and paint a house.

In one year I can go round the world twice.

William

Time Travel

What to do

* It is obviously important for children to develop an awareness of time – and fascinating to discover how they perceive it.

* A starting point here is to put up all those seven periods of time in a random jumble and invite children to sequence them from shortest to longest.

* Once the correct order is established, the question then becomes, "What can you do in each one of them?"

* Children write down the seven line-openings and continue each one describing something they believe they could do in that time.

* Structured as above, the sentences give you a chance to check on the writers' use of the **capital letter** '*I*': first, as the beginning to each sentence and second, as the first-person pronoun.

Can I Just Ask You ...?

O Dandelion

'O dandelion, yellow as gold,
what do you do all day?'
    'I just wait here in the tall green grass
    till the children come to play.'

'O dandelion, yellow as gold,
what do you do all night?'
    'I wait and wait till the cool dews fall
    and my hair grows long and white.'

'And what do you do when your hair is white
and the children come to play?'
    'They take me up in their dimpled hands
    And blow my hair away.'

                          Anon

Can I just ask you lamppost?

How tall are you?
How long have you been outside my house?
Where did you get made?
Do you like switching your light on?
Do you like getting wet?
Who is your best friend?
Will you fall over?

                          Shaun

Can I Just Ask You ...?

What to do

* Any parent will tell you that one of the things children like doing is asking questions. Lots of them. When they come to school, this can change, as we grown-ups take over the question asking. This writing activity seeks to redress the imbalance – and at the same time have young writers get used to using **question marks** to end their questions.

* Talking to a weed, whatever next! But it is one of the strengths of 'O Dandelion' that it opens up so many fresh possibilities for who or what might be asked questions – animals (living or extinct), objects, things in outer space, buildings, volcanoes – anything, in fact, that a child is interested in and wants to know more about.

* There is real fun to be had from reading 'O Dandelion', not least because it is a plant and a lifecycle every child will recognise. The question-and-answer structure of the poem also allows you to focus on the need for **question marks** and **full stops** in the alternating couplets.

* Begin by asking writers to put down the title above, ending with their choice of what they wish to ask questions of. This will also get a first question mark in place as a reminder!

* Children then go on to ask all and any questions they can think of.

Differentiation suggestion

* More confident writers might be asked then to write answers to their questions, in the manner of 'O Dandelion'. If they do use that poem as a model, you'll need to make it quite clear that no rhyming is needed. Alternatively, like Shaun, they can leave their questions unanswered and their chosen subject silent and mysterious.

Would You Rather ...?

> Would you rather grow wings and fly to an island or eat toast and jam all day?
>
> Would you rather wear pyjamas to come to school or live at the North Pole with Father Christmas?
>
> Would you rather hold a warm rabbit or play loud music in a rock band?
>
> Would you rather build a snowman in the garden or meet a dragon on the way home from school?
>
> Or do you now want to go outside for a good run around?
>
> Stacey and Lola

What to do

* This idea is inspired by John Burningham's wonderfully stimulating picture book *Would You Rather ...*, first published back in 1978.

* If you have a copy – either in its original or its newly republished guise – sharing it with your children is the obvious way into the activity. If not, then showing them how the repeated sentence pattern works will suffice.

* In the picture book, readers are offered multiple choices on each page; here, they will just get two.

* In each compound sentence, readers are offered their two choices, the first beginning *Would you rather;* the second, linked by the **conjunction** *or* – and ending with the obligatory **question mark**.

* Print out the sheet of commonly used **verbs** on page 46 and cut it up to make a set of 32 separate words. This will at once build variety into the children's writing.

* Give writers a set of verbs, either face down or in a container, as a lucky dip.

* For each line they want to write, they take two verbs and start the line by writing *Would you rather* followed by one of their verbs plus, as in the girls' example above, some details and development. Once done, they write *or* plus their second verb and complete the sentence, again with some enlivening details.

* For a final line, writers are simply asked what they want to do now. They can write this in their own way or use John Burningham's opening to his final line with *Or perhaps you would rather ...*

Would You Rather ...?

be	watch	stay	give
go	hear	hold	sit
open	win	have	make
see	swim	buy	become
get	find	run	live
meet	read	grow	walk
build	fly	ask	follow
drive	wear	play	eat

That's Not My Question!

Where do you go on holiday?
Cheesy pizza.
What's your favourite colour?
Yorkshire.
What is your best tea?
November.
When is your birthday?
Yellow.

Group made piece

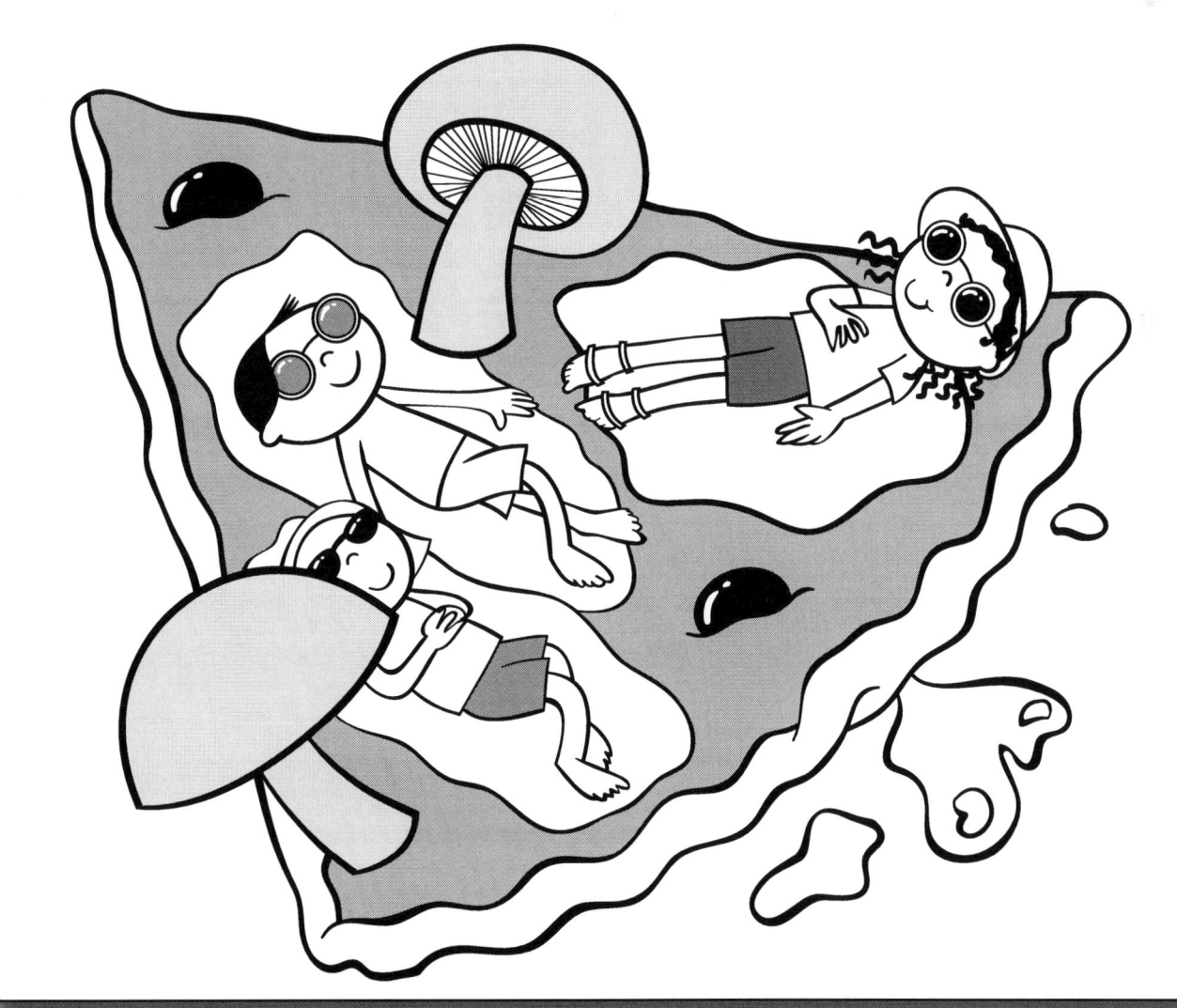

That's Not My Question!

What to do

* This is a party game, adapted for the classroom to appeal to young children's love of the absurd. It also gets them working on their **sentence punctuation**.

* Start by telling the children that they are going to be asking each other some **questions**. The idea is to find out some interesting facts about each other – so no questions wanting only 'yes' or 'no' answers. Ask for suggestions and maybe put some key words up to stimulate ideas.

* Organise children into groups of 4-6 around tables. Each child playing needs a pencil and two strips of paper. On one strip they write 'Q'; they write 'A' on the other.

* On the 'Q' strip each player writes their question. When all players in a group are ready, they pass their 'Q' strips to the person on their left.

* Players now write their answer to the question they receive on their 'A' strip.

* Next, tell the players to turn their 'A' strips over and pass this upside-down strip to the person on their left.

* Now, children take turns round the table to turn their 'A' strips over and read aloud the question in front of them and the absurd answer. Pause for hoots of laughter.

* Finally, ask the children to arrange the questions and answers in this order down the middle of the table. As a group, they must now work to make sure all the necessary **capital letters**, **full stops** and **question marks** are in place.

Too!

I like sticky toffee pudding with custard.
I like fizzy water with an umbrella on top too!

I like my granny's cat Wilfred.
I like dolphins with their smooth skin too!

I like going on the swings with my friend Nicole in the park.
I like dressing up in my bedroom too!

Hayley (extract)

Too!

What to do

* That is just the first half of Hayley's poem about some of her favourite things.

* Offer that one-word title with its **exclamation mark** straight away to establish how it should be read and said.

* Having the same opening to every line gives the poem its basic shape and pulse – and helps the writers get over that great hurdle of how to begin.

* Rather than a simple sequence of random ideas, the 'likes' are paired up into two thematically related lines, with the whole poem presented as a sequence of linked **couplets**.

* In the extract on page 49, Hayley was asked first for a favourite food and then a favourite drink; next a pet animal and a wild animal; then something to enjoy doing with friends and something to do on her own.

* Other suggestions for pairs of lines include:

    + favourite places – one indoors, one outdoors

    + favourite clothes – in summer and in winter

    + favourite reading material and favourite film, TV show or computer game

    + favourite day of the week and favourite time of year.

* When the children have finished writing, it's time to focus on the punctuation, especially the need for a **full stop** after each first line and an **exclamation mark** after the '*too*' in the second line. Remind children that the **pronoun** *I* is always capitalised. (In this case it appears at the start of a sentence, so there are double reasons to capitalise it.)

* In shared readings of the poems, ensure children make each second line that little bit more excited and thus a proper exclamation.

The Mouse's Tale

Hickory, dickory, dock!
The mouse ran up the clock.
The clock struck one,
the mouse ran down.
Hickory, dickory, dock

The Mouse's Tale

What to do

✳ Start by reading the rhyme together – though maybe the children can say it with their eyes shut!

✳ Display the rhyme for all to see. Look at some of the surface features:

  ◆ the **exclamation mark** in line 1 – but not in line 5. How does the punctuation tell us how to read each line?

  ◆ the nonsense words

  ◆ the end-**rhymes**: *dock/clock* and *one/down*

  ◆ The children might also spot the internal rhyme of *Hickory, dickory*.

✳ Explain that now we know what happened at one o'clock, we might now go on to see what happens at two o'clock, three o'clock, etc.

✳ The rhyme begins with the mouse running up a clock. Can the children suggest other things it might run up? *A ladder, a wall, a leg*, etc. Collect and note down all their ideas.

✳ Remind the children of the opening rhyme and choose an item from the collection to make a new opening rhyme. If the choice is '*ladder*', you now need a rhyming nonsense word, so the first two lines of verse 2 could become:

  Hickory, dickory, dadder!
  The mouse ran up the ladder.

✳ Line 3 is obviously T*he clock struck two*. Ask for words that rhyme with *two*. Make a collection – *zoo, shoe, toodle-oo*, etc. Next ask the children to suggest ways of making a sentence that ends in any of those rhyme words. Maybe *the mouse went to the zoo* or *hid in a shoe* or *said toodle-oo*. Add the agreed rhyming couplet to your opening lines; repeat that new first line and verse 2 is complete.

✳ You can now go on to three o'clock and as far as ten or twelve o'clock. You can work as a whole class; alternatively, small groups or pairs of children can work on a chosen thing to climb and hour, making a verse each.

✳ Once complete, all the rhymes can be collected together in a big picture book, good for teaching counting and telling the time to younger children – and also great for performing and reading aloud.

Daze of the Week

Water

Ear

Dog

Nest

Eye

Snowball

Drum

Astronaut

Yogurt

Group made piece

Daze of the Week

What to do

* No sooner have children learned to recite the days of the week in order, than they have to start to recognise them and spell them correctly.

* And what a strange bunch of unruly spellings they are! None more so than *Wednesday*. Here therefore is an activity to get children to engage in detail with each of the days by introducing them to **acrostic poems**.

* Put simply, an acrostic is a piece of writing in which the first letters of each line spell a word. In these acrostics, there will only be a single word in each line as shown in the example on page 53.

* The purpose is to have children look long and hard at the days' seven spellings by composing an acrostic for each day.

* This makes a good whole class project, so prepare by writing each day onto a separate strip of card. Divide the class into seven small groups and give one strip to each group.

* Each group needs a sheet of paper to share and a picture dictionary.

* Ask each group to select one member to rewrite their given day vertically down the left side of their paper – with the rest looking on to see there are no errors.

* Groups now open their dictionaries at each of their day's letters and from there choose one word to form the growing acrostic.

* You can let groups choose words freely or specify that they choose **nouns**, **verbs** or **adjectives**.

* Once the acrostics are composed and shared, they can be incorporated into posters for classroom display.

Rhyme Time

> Fire! Fire! said Mrs Dyer.
> Where? Where? said Mrs Dare.
> Up the town, said Mrs Brown.
> Any damage? said Mrs Gamage.
> None at all, said Mrs Hall.

What to do

* No doubt about it – young children love **rhyme**! So much so that they often firmly believe any unrhymed poem isn't really a poem at all. Well, that's an issue for another day; right now, let's indulge them!

* The rhyme above is a popular, much anthologised piece, and a real joy to read out loud.

* However, another approach is to make a copy of the version on page 56, cut it into ten strips, give them a good shuffle and ask pairs or groups first to match the rhyming half lines and second put the five full lines into their correct order.

* Now we come to the children's own writing. As much as they love reading and hearing rhyme, writing their own rhymed pieces almost always ends disappointingly. In our poem, however, all the rhymes come simply from the speakers' names. There are no limits on the names they can use or invent, solving the rhyming problem at a stroke.

* Here are two approaches.

    1. You could improvise lines all together before children start their own writing: Offer some new opening lines, such as *Rain! Rain! said Mrs Payne* or *Look out! Look out! said Mrs Stout*. Ask children now to write their own four lines to add to a given opening – with four fresh characters and bits of speech.

    Or

    2. Keep the first two lines of the original poem and write any number of new rhymes to make it a longer piece. Line 3 might become *Orchard Road, said Mrs Toad* or *In the wood, said Mrs Hood*.

* Simple as the rhyme is, it also offers opportunities to look at key bits of punctuation: **full stops**, **exclamation marks** and **question marks** as well as **capital letters** for names and titles.

Rhyme Time

Fire! Fire!	said Mrs Dyer.
Where? Where?	said Mrs Dare.
Up the town,	said Mrs Brown.
Any damage?	said Mrs Gamage.
None at all,	said Mrs Hall.

Guided Fantasy

The Spiked Dragon

China. 1.30pm. Hot. A door of stone. The walls are rough. Smooth ceiling. Footsteps. Rocking of binoculars. Rumbling of stomach. The air smells like steam. The dragon has spikes on its back and a tail as long as a car. The dragon sounds like a motorbike and a car joined together. I look at the spikes on its back, they are as big as a jar of paint. The eye was as big as 4,000,000 ice cubes and he blinked.

Lois

Guided Fantasy

What to do

* Some of the most popular picture books of recent years are guided fantasies – where the author takes the reader, as well as some of the story's characters, on a journey and an adventure. Julia Donaldson's *The Gruffalo* and Michael Rosen's *We're Going on a Bear Hunt* are two prime examples.

* For her story, Lois and her class were taken on a fantasy journey of their own, with an adult doing the guiding. In this, and as an example of what this approach can achieve, Lois and her class went dragon hunting. Here is an outline of that particular journey:

* Children have paper and pencils and are told they are all going on an adventure – in this case a search for a dragon. They are told they will be stopping at points along the way and there they will be asked to write. Here are those points and the instructions to the writers (Some children might like to close their eyes whenever you stop to speak):

    + To begin, write down where you are, the time of day and what the weather is like.

    + We reach the entrance to a cave. Write down what it is like, especially to touch.

    + Can you hear or smell anything? How do you feel inside?

    + You get your first sight of the dragon. It is asleep. What does it look like? Can you hear it making any noises?

    + You go closer to look at one bit of the dragon. Write about the bit you choose.

    + As you stand there, the dragon moves just a little bit. Write down what moves.

* Always wait for the last child to finish writing before moving on to the next stage.

* This model can be used for any adventure journey you, or the children, choose.

Differentiation suggestion

* Writing done in this way is always a first draft. The teacher can then use the drafts to discuss SPaG issues – such as that shift in tense at the very end of 'The Spiked Dragon' – without diminishing the power of the writing, thus introducing the habit of proofreading. Differentiation here comes from each child's outcome, and not from the task itself, which should be the same for all.

That Does It!

High does it.
Night does it.
Light does it.
But eventually does not.

                Thomas

Edge does it
and badge does it
and bridge does it
and fridge does it
but principality does not!

                Billy

That Does It!

What to do

* It's soon clear what the listed words do in each of those puzzle-pieces. They each feature one of the spelling patterns listed in the appendix on spelling to the Key Stage 1 English curriculum.

* The advantage of activities like these is that they can be used for any of the 70+ patterns required to be taught by teachers of Years 1 and 2.

* Just choose one or more patterns you want children to focus on and ask them to make a collection of all the words they can find that fit.

* Children can list each word, plus *does it* to make simple sentences, like Thomas in Year 1. Or they can use the **conjunction** *and* to make one long compound sentence, like Billy in Year 2.

* Whatever their approach, they should then end their piece with one word that definitely doesn't fit the pattern – perhaps a favourite word, one they use a lot, the longest word they know. Encourage them to use a word that is a real contrast: something to let the writer show off their vocabulary and give the piece a final flourish.

* Pieces featuring different patterns can then be written large to make attractive and instructive classroom posters.

Let's Write a Musical

What to do

✳ There's an old comic song from Liverpool, called 'We're off in a motor car'. You can easily find performances of it on YouTube. The original song involved being chased around the city by a large number of police officers.

✳ The two-line chorus is a genuine earworm, and the chorus is all you need for your musical. It's an ideal activity for a whole class, working all together and in small groups. And it's huge fun!

✳ To begin, change the second line of the original chorus to:

Ten lions are after us and they don't know where we are!

✳ Show – and sing! – your chorus until everyone can join in. Explain that they are going to use it to compose a brand-new musical.

✳ Tell the children that they are going to be chased, not just by ten lions, but by lots of animals.

✳ Explain that the musical is going to be in the form of a countdown and so we'll need eight more different animals to get down to '*Two*'. This is where children might break into small groups to think of, note down and offer fresh animals. So, the sequence might be *Nine rabbits ... / Eight camels ...* and so on.

✳ Repeat the first line of the chorus before each countdown line. Add the eight animals to the text and finally offer the concluding, climactic line:

One teacher is after us and (s)he DOES know where we are!

✳ That's the basic activity but given such a simple – and therefore flexible – tune, more can be done with it, with older or more able children writing in small groups to compose each verse, with extra writing challenges. So, for example:

- ✦ Add an **adjective** to each animal/**noun**: *Ten hungry lions*, etc.

- ✦ Make a really comical, **alliterative** version, based on the initial letter sounds of the numbers such as *Ten tellies ... / Nine nighties ...* Add alliterating **adjectives** here too.

- ✦ Ask for two adjectives for each noun and make one into an adverb to make a sequence of noun phrases, for example: *Ten happily hairy puppies ... / Nine smartly spotty crocodiles ...*

✳ Once complete, it can be sung and performed live and the text made into a large picture book.

Opposites Attract

Small Box – Big Monster

The box is small.
The box is little.
The box is tiny.
The box is titchy.
The box is teeny weeny.
The box is minute.

But

the monster is big.
The monster is large.
The monster is huge.
The monster is massive.
The monster is enormous.
The monster is ginormous.

And the monster is in the box!

Extract from class-made piece

Opposites Attract

What to do

* This version of the activity is for the whole class, leading to a dramatic performance-piece. However, it can also be done by individual children.

* It revolves around words with the same or similar meanings (**synonyms**) and words with opposite meanings (**antonyms**). Children aren't expected to add the terms to their terminology bank until Year 6, but children in Key Stage 1 understand the concept perfectly well.

* Looking at words related in meaning can be an excellent way to develop the range and precision of children's vocabularies.

* Divide the class into two halves. Ask one half to make a list of words they know that mean '*small*' and to write all their offered synonyms onto a large sheet of paper. The other half of the class should do the same, but looking for synonyms for '*big*'. This is a good opportunity to introduce a thesaurus to children.

* When the two collections are made, cut each one up into its constituent words and ask the children to help you make two word-ladders, ordering the words downwards to mean ever smaller and ever bigger. There are no definitely right and wrong answers here, and the discussion can get very lively and sophisticated.

* Once an order for each ladder is agreed, glue the words down the right-hand sides of two more large sheets.

* Explain to the children that they are now going to be writing a large-scale performance piece, called 'Small Box – Big Monster'.

* Take the sheet of synonyms for '*small*' first and before each of the adjectives, the children or you write *The box is ….* So, as the example shows, the first line becomes *The box is small*, and the second maybe, *The box is little*, and so on down the page.

* Repeat this process with the synonyms for '*big*' and this time before each adjective write, *The monster is ….* So, as the example shows, the first line becomes *The monster is big*, and the second perhaps *The monster is large*, and so on down the page. Therefore, as the box gets smaller, the monster gets bigger!

* To connect the two sections, add the **conjunction** *But*. Finally, at the foot of this page, to make your dramatic ending, add, *And the monster is in the box!*

* Confident writers can go on to write their own Opposites Attract pieces, again with a thesaurus, using pairs of adjectival antonyms with appropriate nouns. For example: dry home/wet day; bad test/good mark; cold day/hot soup; quiet beach/loud sea.

Simply Similes

I am a space alien!

My name is Asejm.

I am black and purple and ginormous.

I hum like a bee in a forest.

I walk like a cow on a farm.

I shout like 10 babies.

I dash like me buying Pokémon cards.

I live on planet Hat.

James

Simply Similes

What to do

* Begin by asking the children to imagine that, as well as being themselves and human, they are also – a space alien! They are now going to write to introduce and describe their new outer-space selves.

* First, therefore, they write the title, *I am a space alien!* This gives you an opportunity to introduce the **exclamation mark** and explain what it does.

* Each writer needs a space alien name. They make this by jumbling up the letters of their own first name. They write this anagrammed name in an opening line like James' example above.

* For the second line, writers give at least two details about their appearance – colour, size, shape, character – using the **conjunction** *and* between each detail they use.

* Explain that now they are going to write about how, in their alien form, they make noises and how they move about. To do this, write *'speak'* and *'move'* for all to see – and create two scatter diagrams with all the **verbs** the children can tell you that fit around either diagram. You can perhaps introduce a thesaurus here, adding any fresh words to the diagrams you feel might be useful.

* Children now begin the four main lines of their poems. Each line starts *I*, followed by four of the verbs from the diagrams – two for *speak* and two for *move*.

* After selecting and writing down each verb, children add *like* to start a **simile**. They then complete the line with a comparison that they feel fits the verb well. Remind the children that now they are space aliens, their sounds and movements can be very different to their earthly noises and actions. Encourage the strange and unlikely to make a clear contrast with their human selves.

* As a closing line, children finish their poems of introduction by naming the planet on which they live. This might be an anagram again, of their actual hometown, or, like James, a place wholly of their own inventing.

Just Because

Cheetahs
    I like them.
    Ask me why.
        Because they run really fast.
        Because they've got spots and their tails
                      are really long.
        Because they have sharp claws and
                      sharp teeth.
        Because they have good hearing ears.
        Because they're sneaky.
        Because.
        Because. That's why
I like cheetahs.
                              Austin

Chameleons
    I like them.
    Ask me why.
        Because they can change colour.
        Because they can blend in.
        Because they have strong claws.
        Because their tongues are so long.
        Because they have curly tails.
        Because they're good at climbing trees.
        Because they have big eyes that
                      go round and round.
        Because.
        Because. That's why
I like chameleons.
                              Hector

Just Because

What to do

✳ The starting point for this activity is a well-known poem called 'Giraffes'. It's by Mary Ann Hoberman and you can easily find it by a quick internet search. If you're familiar with the poem already, then you'll know exactly where Austin and Hector got their inspiration from.

✳ It is a perfect model for young writers to borrow, as the boys' pieces show. In fact, if you don't have time to seek out Hoberman's original, then 'Cheetahs' and 'Chameleons' will serve perfectly well as the models for your own writers to imitate.

✳ Having read and enjoyed the detail and structure of whichever poems you've picked, ask the children to choose one animal they really like and want to concentrate on to celebrate in their own poems.

✳ It's ideal if the writers can see the featured poem(s) as they work, either via printed copies or large screen. This is because, once they have written their own title, those poems give writers all the structural help (and punctuation!) they'll need. Each line they write just has to add something fresh to the growing poem. They can rhyme some lines if they wish, and they can have as many lines beginning Because as they want. There has to be just enough detail in each line to make a reader enjoy their chosen animal as much as they do.

✳ Born in New England in 1930, Mary Ann Hoberman was US Children's Poet Laureate from 2008-2011. In her poem she has a strong closing detail to complete her giraffe. This device was pointed out to Austin and Hector and so they too saved a favourite detail till last.

✳ Finally, of course, poems inspired by 'Giraffes' (or 'Cheetahs' or 'Chameleons') don't have to be about animals. Other subjects, such as 'Weather', 'Places', 'Seasons', 'People', are plentiful.

Once Upon a Time

Once I was a pencil but now I am a cloud.
Once I was a cake but now I am a squirrel.
Once I was a seesaw but now I am a bell.
Once I was a button but now I am a disco.
Once I was a doctor but now I am a tree.

Iris and Vivien

Once Upon a Time

What to do

* This activity derives from an idea in the classic book *Wishes, Lies and Dreams* by the poet Kenneth Koch, an account of his time getting New York children excited about writing.

* Ask children to work in pairs on a joint piece, sharing writing duties. It helps if each pair can have access to a picture dictionary.

* Show the writers the repeated pattern of each line: *Once I was a ... but now I am a ...* with the **conjunction** *but* joining two **simple sentences** into one **compound sentence**.

* Pairs agree who will write first and that person begins by writing the sentence opening, followed by any object of their choosing.

* The partner now takes over by writing the second half of the sentence plus a new object. To make the poem interesting, the writer should aim to make their new object different to the first one. It should also begin with a different letter of the alphabet, as in Iris and Vivien's' *pencil* and *cloud* above.

* The first writer then starts a new line with a fresh object starting with the same letter as the second item in line 1. So, *cloud* and *cake*.

* The challenge to the writers is to feature different letters in every line they make.

* Emphasise that writers are working as a pair and encourage them to go hunting for ideas at any time in their dictionary, always looking for variety in their choices. For every line they write, they'll be getting some good experience of using a **verb** consistently in its **present** and **past** tense.

Differentiation suggestions

* Less confident writers should be encouraged to write just three- or four-line pieces and to focus on good word choices and enjoyable contrasts.

* A good challenge for the most able children is to produce a poem of 13 lines, featuring 26 different items, each one starting with a different letter of the alphabet.

Special Senses

My real nose smells popcorn in the cinema
   but my special nose breathes in air at the North Pole.
My real ears hear next door's dog bark
   but my special ears listen to aliens on Jupiter.
My real mouth tastes red grapes
   but my special mouth eats strawberry ice cream in Africa.
My real eyes see Alfie next to me
   but my special eyes watch sharks underwater.
My real hands hold a snowball
   but my special hands stroke a tiger.

                                        Rory

Special Senses

What to do

* The American poet and teacher Ron Padgett asked children to imagine they had what he called a 'third eye'. They would then write poems describing what they could see with it. His rule to them was that this third eye could see anything and everything – except the things their ordinary eyes could see.

* This activity takes that idea further and asks children to imagine that, as well as having their everyday five senses, they have five more special senses. These work like Ron Padgett's third eye and you're free to interpret that rule of his however you wish.

* Start by discussing the five senses humans have and then introduce the notion of the five special senses. Children always find the idea intriguing and will happily dream up and describe experiences these new powers will grant them.

* As Rory's poem demonstrates, each sense and special sense feature in five **compound sentences**, using the **conjunction** *but*. It might help if you show how the repeated sentence pattern will work by creating one or two examples all together ahead of any individual writing.

* Because of the poem's repeated pattern, you might usefully introduce the idea of getting variety into the poems through their vocabulary. So, for example, children can have 'real' and 'special' senses, or maybe 'ordinary' and 'magic', or 'everyday' and 'extra'.

* The **verbs** in each line offer real possibilities for variation. So:

    + The eyes: see; look at; watch; stare at
    + The ears: hear; listen to; catch
    + The nose: smells; sniffs; breathes in
    + The mouth: tastes; eats;. drinks; swallows
    + The hands: touch;. feel; hold; stroke

* Encourage writers to keep the activity of each normal sense as ordinary as possible. This makes the contrast with the special sense all the more noticeable.

There's Always a But

> **Doctor Daft's Inventions**
>
> A window made of rubber.
> You can't see through it but it will not break when your ball hits it.
>
> A spoon made of ice.
> It will make a hot drink cool but will also disappear fast.
>
> A bridge made of glass.
> You can see lots underneath you but it might break as you go over it.
>
> Owen (extract)

What to do

* In the Key Stage 1 science curriculum, children are asked to think about a range of materials and their suitability or otherwise for certain purposes and are 'encouraged to think about unusual and creative uses for everyday materials'.

* There are very few made things in the world that don't come with advantages and disadvantages and, as you can see above, Owen has made unlikely combinations of materials and objects to see if they offer any gains. He presents his findings, styling himself as Doctor Daft and offering an advantage and a disadvantage each time.

* A lot of talk should precede any writing as children consider the possibilities of any number of unlikely products (including some from fiction: the little pigs' houses, Cinderella's glass slippers) such as wooden clothes, cardboard boats, elastic cars and so on.

* Ask the children to see themselves as crazy inventors and, as a first task, give themselves a title (Professor, Doctor) and a suitable name to follow.

* Writers choose a number of unlikely items from the discussion and their own imagining. For each one they should first write a phrase to say what it is and what it is made from.

* Next, they write an evaluation for each item, presented in the form of a **compound sentence**, using the **conjunction** *but* to set up the two contrary outcomes.

* Products can be presented finally in the form of advertising posters and promotional leaflets.

Sometimes

Sometimes at playtime I walk in the playground with my friends.
Sometimes atplaytimeweallrunaroundandshoutlikecrazy!

Sometimes the wind doesn't blow at all. The trees are still.
Sometimes astormcomestheskygoesblackandeverythingcrashesabout!

Sometimes fireworks just make lots of sparkles.
Sometimes fireworksgobangreallyloudandmakemejump!

Charlotte, Seb and Carla

Sometimes

What to do

✳ It's obviously important that young writers learn the importance of **separating words** in their writing – principally to help the reader make sense quickly.

✳ However, once children have got the hang of the need for leaving spaces, it can sometimes be a lot of fun squashing words up together – not to go backwards with their writing skills, but rather to show they understand about word separation through the very act of ignoring it.

✳ The purpose of the word-squash is solely to make particular effects on the page. You can see this in the examples on page 73, where the children create the speed, energy and racket of their scenes through the playful tumult of each of their second lines, made deliberately tricky to read.

✳ The idea can be tried in describing in two lines any scene which can offer a marked contrast. For example:

- an animal – at rest/moving quickly
- car – on drive/on busy road
- rain – gentle shower/downpour
- rocket – on launch pad/ lifting off
- baby – sleeping/ awake and hungry
- haunted house – silent/ sudden spooky noise

✳ Each line starts *Sometimes*. The first line spaces words conventionally and the second line squeezes them together for the desired effect.

Warning: young writers can find ignoring spaces between words difficult to do consistently – which only goes to prove how well they are internalising the necessary convention!

Countdown to ...

Home time

10 Tidy all our things away.

9 Sit on the carpet with our legs crossed.

8 Listen to the end of day story.

7 Walk to pegs outside classroom.

6 Get coat and go back to classroom.

5 See grownups outside the window.

4 Get letter to take home.

3 Put coats on.

2 Say bye to Mrs Skerritt.

1 Walk outside to meet all the grown-ups.

0 Home time!

Group made piece

Countdown to ...

What to do

* Of course, it doesn't have to be home time; it can be a countdown to any event, whether an everyday one such as playtime or the weekend, or a special occasion such as a birthday party or holiday.

* Whatever the topic, the process is the same. Once given the countdown topic, children in groups need some slips of paper for each of them to write on.

* Each child must take a slip and write just one thing they must do before they reach the actual event. They should think of their writing as instructions to others (called **commands** in the National Curriculum), telling them what they have to do. They keep taking slips and writing their ideas in whatever order they think of them.

* For sentences like these, writers need to put the **verb** – sometimes called a **bossy verb** first. All the slips created by the group are then pooled and sorted, with duplicates rejected, and discussions held as to what might be missing. A total of ten points isn't essential, but it makes a clear challenge and gets them thinking in greater detail.

* When writers have written all the points they can think of, they sort their slips of commands into order: from first down to last. When they are satisfied with their sequencing, they number each one down to 1. They add one last slip, this time marked 0 plus the actual event – with a final **exclamation mark**!

Differentiation suggestion

* Confident writers can be stimulated by this to produce their own independent countdowns, possibly doing a mind-dump of random ideas as a draft, which they can put into a satisfying sequence by numbering the dump, before writing a final, numbered draft.

Then and Now

The end of a school day

Then
We were tidying our things away.
We were all sitting down on the carpet.
We were listening to the story.
Mrs Haslam was reading The Twits to us.
We were putting on our coats and hats.

Now
We are walking outside.
We are saying bye to Mrs Haslam.
Mummies are pushing buggies.
We are crossing the road.
We are going home for hot chocolate and a snack.

Elliott and Pavel

Then and Now

What to do

* As you can see, the focus here is the **progressive verb** form – the one ending *-ing* – with the added element being that in part 1, the verb is in the **past tense** (*Then*) and in part 2 it is in the **present tense** (*Now*). The objective is to have children write consistently and purposefully in the appropriate tense.

* The way into this activity is to offer the children a two-part sequence from the school day, such as the one above. Similar *Then/Now* sequences include:

  + arriving at school/coming into the classroom
  + morning break outside/class time
  + end of the morning/lunch time

* Whatever the topic of the chosen sequence, children need to see the task in its two parts: past and present.

Differentiation suggestions

* For less confident writers, a target of one or two pairs of *Then/Now* lines will get them trying out the grammar of each sentence pattern; more confident children will think of more.

* Less confident children might also find it easier to write about episodes well into the past for the *Then* – for example, their last birthday, a school trip, or holiday – to provide a greater contrast with the *Now* of the current school day.

* They should make a quick note of their thoughts and ideas, under the two headings: *Then* and *Now*. Explain that they will now be converting their notes into sentences, set into their correct chronological order. Each sentence will be using the *-ing* verb form, with the *Then* events in the past tense and the *Now* events in the present tense.

* It is clearly important for writers to understand how useful the progressive verb form is in this piece of work. Its general purpose is to describe things going on for some time. Here, therefore, its use lets readers imagine a sequence of events as if they were actually watching them happen.

Let's Go Ladder-ing!

Building with Lego.

    Eating cake icing.

        Watching Star Wars movies.

            Playing in warm sunshine.

                Seeing colourful rainbows.

                    Lifting heavy things.

                        Drinking bath water.

                            Climbing too high.

                                Eating mashed potato.

                                    Waiting.

                                        Tomasz

Let's Go Ladder-ing!

What to do

* Tomasz's ladder of the things he likes doing and the things he doesn't like doing is on page 79. They are ordered from his favourite to his least favourite thing to do.

* Begin by talking all together about favourite and least favourite activities.

* Ask the children to write collections of their own. They should aim for 6-10 items, putting them down just in the order they think of them.

* Emphasise throughout that they are writing only about things they do and so there has to be a **verb**, a 'doing word', to start each of their items. Writers can imagine themselves actually doing each item and therefore the verbs will need to be in the **progressive** form, with the suffix *-ing* added to the root word.

* Once writing time is up, ask the children to look at their items and see how many different verbs they have used. If they have repeats of verbs, ask if they or other children can suggest alternatives to keep the writing varied – and show off the range of words they know.

* Writers now start to sequence their collections of ideas from the most liked to the most disliked. Some children will find this process easier if they have been asked to write their original items each on a separate strip of paper, so they can then manipulate their strips into order; other children might want to number each of their items on the initial draft in order of their preference.

* Once writers have their items satisfactorily sequenced, however they have done so, they can now write their final drafts.

Poems for Presents

A Poem for You

Today I am not doing hard sums.
    I am not chasing Gethin in the playground.
        I am not dancing to Dance Monkey.
            I am not riding my bike 100 miles.
                I am not meeting Iron Man for a new adventure.

        Today I am writing this poem for you!

                Fergal

Poems for Presents

What to do

* As much as children like receiving presents, they like giving them too. This is a simple way for young writers to compose a poem as a gift specifically for someone. It's also a way for them to practise using the **present progressive verb** form several times!

* Start by asking the children to tell you anything they are not doing right now. At first, they might think it's a trick question, but pretty soon they'll be offering all sorts of things – especially with some encouragement – to suggest ideas beyond the obvious.

* Write up a few of their suggestions and use these to point out the consistent use of the progressive verb form – and the way we use it to describe things happening (or, in this context, not happening) at this very moment.

* Now ask them to write as many sentences as they can – each on a fresh line, and each using the progressive form – with their own choices of things they are not doing.

* Ask them to start with the ordinary and obvious things and add evermore outlandish ideas as they progress. Some children might benefit from having strips of paper on which to write each idea separately, so they can then order and re-order these ideas until satisfied.

* You can introduce the final 'twist' line whenever you're ready. It uses the exact same verb form minus the negative and ends with the flourish of an **exclamation mark**.

* Authors regularly dedicate their books to particular people. If you can show some examples, it will help the children write their own dedication to place at the head of their writing.

* Alternatively, the poems can be included in cards for special occasions such as Mother's Day and Christmas.

Body Beautiful

> Brow brinky,
> eye winky,
> chin choppy,
> cheek cherry,
> mouth merry.

What to do

* There are lots of versions of this little nursery rhyme, and they all have one thing in common: the **adjectives** come after the **nouns**. French, Italian, Spanish have this order all the time, but in English we customarily put the adjective before the noun. We have a 'red wheelbarrow' not a 'wheelbarrow red'.

* This swapping of the normal English order means that in those five brief **noun phrases**, the adjectives become all the more noticeable. Our tiny rhyme can therefore become a useful means of introducing adjectives and their purpose to children.

* The poem has a mix of **rhyme** – *brinky/ winky* – and **alliteration** – *choppy/ cherry*. It also uses both known – *merry* – and invented – *brinky* – **adjectives**. However, they all share the **suffix** *-y*, which provides the regular rhythm and rhyme.

* Every version of the rhyme has the same five basic lines – so what about extending the rhyme to include the whole body? As the original has that playful mix of words, you can carry on in the same vein. Begin by inviting the children to list body parts going down from neck to feet.

* Next, after each body part (**noun**), they need to add their chosen adjective, ending in *-y*.

Differentiation suggestions

* The idea offers lots of opportunities for linguistic play and challenge for the more able: the adjective can rhyme with the one before; it can alliterate with the one before; it can be a known adjective; or it can be a made-up one. So, for example, they might make:

  > neck nippy,
  > chest cheeky,
  > arms addy,
  > hands handy,
  > fingers findy,
  > all the way down to, maybe, toes tickly.

* The writers now have a list-poem and so they'll need to add a **comma** at the end of each **noun phrase** line to separate the items in the list, plus one **full stop** at the very end.

What's My Word?

> To a semi-circle add a circle.
> The same again repeat.
> Add to these a triangle –
> and then you'll have a treat.

What to do

* The answer to the rhyming riddle above is COCOA. Clever, isn't it? But it is a bit of a dead-end as an idea, because most capital letters aren't geometric shapes.

* However, if we imagine the letters of the alphabet as real-world objects, then there are a lot more possibilities.

* Start by sharing the riddle and its solution with the children and then ask them to suggest things that each capital letter looks like. For 'A' you might get an arrowhead, a volcano, a pyramid, Toblerone, and so on. Agree together a favourite idea for each letter and so build up your collection of objects for letters, all the way to 'Z' which could be a swan, or lightning, or …

* To write their own riddles, children can copy the style of the original rhyme or simply write each letter-object on a fresh line. No rhyming necessary!

* Here is a one-word riddle made by a group of children after studying that original rhyme. They opted to have a new line for each letter. This makes the writing a clear sequence of instructions as well as an entertaining riddle. To help them, they were introduced to some useful sequencing **adverbs**, First, Now, etc. The answer, if you need it, is at the foot of the page.

What's My Word?
First get a hammer.
Add an old comb.
Now get a volcano.
Next put in one new moon.
Then find a bed.
Add another old comb.
Finish with a ribbon tied in a bow.

TEACHER

Father William's Diary

You Are Old, Father William

'You are old, Father William,' the young man said,
'And your hair has become very white.
And yet you incessantly stand on your head –
Do you think, at your age, it is right?'

'In my youth,' Father William replied to his son,
'I feared it might injure the brain.
But now that I'm perfectly sure I have none,
Why, I do it again and again.'

'You are old,' said the youth, 'as I mentioned before,
And have grown most uncommonly fat.
Yet you turned a back-somersault in at the door –
Pray, what is the reason for that?'

'In my youth,' said the sage, as he shook his grey locks,
'I kept all my limbs very supple
By the use of this ointment – one shilling the box –
Allow me to sell you a couple?'

'You are old,' said the youth, 'and your jaws are too weak
For anything other than suet.
Yet you finished the goose, with the bones and the beak –
Pray, how did you manage to do it?'

'In my youth,' said the father, 'I took to the law,
And argued each case with my wife.
And the muscular strength, which it gave to my jaw
Has lasted the rest of my life.'

'You are old,' said the youth, 'one would hardly suppose
That your eye was as steady as ever.
Yet you balanced an eel on the end of your nose –
What made you so awfully clever?'

'I have answered three questions, and that is enough,'
Said his father. 'Don't give yourself airs!
Do you think I can listen all day to such stuff?
Be off, or I'll kick you downstairs!'

Lewis Carroll

Father William's Diary

Mother Carolina's Diary

Monday. I walked into town on my hands.
Tuesday. I played on the swings in the park all day.
Wednesday. I climbed up trees backwards.
Thursday. I jumped over the moon like that cow did.
Friday. I balanced on a pencil for one hour.
Saturday. I lifted all my family up in the air.
Sunday. For my lunch I ate ten pizzas and the boxes too.

Father William's Diary

What to do

* Lewis Carroll first published 'You Are Old, Father William' in *Alice's Adventures in Wonderland* in 1865. Although never as well-known as 'Jabberwocky', it is the funnier of the two poems, a product of real comedic genius.

* Begin by enjoying the poem with the children: the way the scene unfolds; the conversation between young man and old; and especially Father William himself, a great comic character: white-haired, overweight, possibly toothless and yet still full of life. How old do they think he might be?

* Focus the children's attention on William's absurd acrobatic feats – standing on his head, somersaulting backwards, balancing an eel on his nose – and also his extraordinary diet.

* Ask the children to now see themselves in old age, not inactive but, like Father William, vital and vigorous, doing the wildest, most adventurous things! Ask them also to imagine Father William kept a diary, in which he recorded what he had got up to every day.

* Have the children see themselves as future Father (or Mother) Williams and imagine that they too keep such a diary telling the tricks they have performed. They are going to write the diary entries for seven days to build, in effect, a short narrative of their week.

* Writers start by writing the appropriate title for them, and below that the days of the week in order.

* Being careful to use the **past tense** throughout, they write their seven diary entries, in which they describe what they have done (or eaten!) each day.

* Remind the children of how varied Father William's tricks were. If they are going to keep their readers entertained through the whole week, they must do the same and come up with a range of escapades, all enjoyably different from one another.

* When proofreading the piece, they should check that they have used **capital letters** for the days of the week and the pronoun *I* and ended each sentence with a **full stop**.

The Museum of Me

Welcome to my museum. Come in. That is the toy kitchen and food for when I played cafes. This is my first Spiderman suit. I got it when I was four. Here is the step I stood on to wash my hands. There is the very first bowl of Coco pops I had for breakfast.

That is the lion I go to see at Chester Zoo. This is my bike I ride in the park. There is the stomp rocket I jump on to make it shoot into the sky. There are the biscuits I make with mummy. Thank you.

Lewis

The Museum of Me

What to do

* This activity needs lots of preparatory talking and listening before any writing happens. The talk will be autobiographical, focussing on the children's lives, past and present, covering such topics as clothes, foods, books and stories, toys, accidents and illnesses, games, friends, places visited.

* Children are now asked to imagine that each of them has a museum all about them: The Museum of Me. This museum holds the objects and experiences of their lives so far.

* They are now going to write an information text, a short guided tour to their museums to show visitors some of what is inside. Most importantly, their tour must include items from both their past and their present lives.

* A homework task to explain to and interview adults on the subject can provide extra material.

* You can offer writers some ways they might meet and greet visitors to their museum, and make them welcome, as Lewis does at the start. He was also taught ways to introduce particular items: *That is*, *Here is*, etc.

* Their writing will now be in two distinct halves: **past** and **present**. Writers should aim to include at least three items for each half. They will need to describe each item in the correct **verb tense** with every item they include giving them useful early experience of handling the two tenses correctly and consistently.

* A story to accompany this activity is 'Life Savings' by Allan Ahlberg. You'll find it in *The Clothes Horse and Other Stories* (Puffin)

When ...

When it's Diwali we light lamps and candles everywhere.
When it's Hanukkah we light our menorah at night.
When it's Christmas we put up the Christmas tree.
When it's Chinese New Year we have fireworks.
When it's Eid we all give presents.

Extract from a class-made piece

When ...

What to do

✳ That extract is just part of a longer piece in which children had explored how many different festivals they all enjoyed – and in the process, found how similar they all are.

✳ That little word *When* has to be one of the most useful of all ways to start a sentence. This is because it can introduce so many subjects for pieces of writing. For example:

- **the days of the week**: *When* it's Monday, *When* it's Tuesday, etc.

  Children write the openings to the seven sentences and complete each one by writing something they do, or something that happens on that particular day.

- **the months of the year**: *When* it's January, *When* it's February, etc.

  Now twelve sentences needed, each one describing one or more features of the different months. With illustrations, this activity can make good calendars.

- **the four seasons**: *When* it's Spring, *When* it's Summer, etc.

  Just four lines, obviously. But children can make longer pieces by repeating the openings and having a fresh focus each time, for example, the weather, favourite activities, animal and plant life.

- **the weather**: *When* it's raining, *When* the sun shines, etc.

  Begin by collecting all the different forms the weather takes. Children complete lines by writing something that happens in each chosen weather. Ask for good details in the writing to bring each weather vividly to life.

- **a mood poem**: *When* I'm happy, *When* I'm tired, etc.

  Begin by discussing and collecting a range of moods they experience. After each line opening, children write to say how each mood makes them feel, what they do when in a particular mood, how they appear to others.

The Twelve Months

> Snowy, Flowy, Blowy,
> Showery, Flowery, Bowery,
> Hoppy, Croppy, Droppy,
> Breezy, Sneezy, Freezy.
>
> George Ellis

What to do

* No, not more dwarves for Snow White, but rather the year defined in twelve adjectives, written by the 18th Century author and cartoonist, George Ellis.

* Young children love reading and listening to rhymes but their own attempts to write in rhyme don't always end well. However, in this activity, we're going to pinch George Ellis's rhymes and put them into a brand-new piece of writing.

* Start by looking at the original rhyme. It is great fun and also an excellent way to talk about the **suffix** -y. The children will recognise most of the words, except maybe *bowery* (from *bower*, a shelter for shade from the sun) and *hoppy* (from *hops*, used to make beer).

* Making a calendar is obviously a good way to learn and practise writing the months of the year and that's what this activity is all about.

* Children start by writing the twelve months in order down the left side of the page, adding the verb *is* after each one.

* From now on, you can make the task as straightforward or demanding as you wish.

* For the simplest approach, that works perfectly well, writers just add two **adjectives** to each of the twelve months, one of their own and George Ellis's original to make, for example: *January is cold and snowy*.

* More demandingly, you can ask writers to include a number of items in each line, linking them with **commas** and the conjunction *and*. These items can be foods, colours, sounds, smells, special events, festivals – whatever fits the particular month – always remembering to finish each line with the correct rhyme word. These additions can be **adjectives**, **nouns** or **phrases** to make, for example: *November is dark, bonfire night, Diwali and sneezy*.

* The final decorated draft of the piece can be turned into a wonderful present if a calendar tab is pasted at the bottom.

What Are Heavy?

What Are Heavy?
>Sea-sand and sorrow.

What are brief?
>Today and tomorrow.

What are frail?
>Spring blossoms and youth.

What are deep?
>The ocean and truth.

>Christina Rossetti

What Are Aloud?

What are aloud?
>A lion's roar and babies crying in their cots.

What are big?
>The playground and an elephant.

What are crumbly?
>A sandcastle as the waves come in and a chocolate cake.

What are dark?
>A bedroom at night and a spooky cave.

>Extract from group-made piece

What Are Heavy?

What to do

* Christina Rossetti published her poem 'What Are Heavy?' almost exactly 150 years ago in a collection of over 100 poems for children she called *Sing-Song*.

* Whatever today's young readers make of some of its detail, its four rhymed lines remain haunting and memorable. And they can be used in a number of ways to stimulate fresh writing.

* That second piece on page 93, for example, is the start to an Abecedarius, featuring 26 different **adjectives**, one for every letter of the alphabet.

* Such an approach can be a good way to introduce and explore the dictionary, with an **adjective** hunt and discussion of which adjectives to choose for each line. You'll need to use *ex* for *x*.

* Young writers need to know they won't be aiming to rhyme their work in the manner of the original poem. Instead, their challenges are:

  + first, to complete the piece with all 26 adjectives in lines ending with **question marks**;

  + second, to come up with two things that each of these adjectives can describe, because of the questions' plural verb *are*. These two things also have to be different from each other – just as in Christina Rossetti's poem. These will be **nouns** – often with details added to expand them into **noun phrases**.

* To acknowledge Christina Rossetti, and to add something extra to any live performances of the new piece, try using the original poem as a chorus, inserted and repeated, perhaps after every five lines of the Abecedarius.

Differentiation suggestion

* For the less able child the opening phrase can be reduced to *What is ...* and the demand therefore for only one item, possibly with an **adjective**.

Making Magic

Abracadabra!
First change a blue car into a bright star!
Then make lots of rain into a fast train!
Next turn thick fog into a crazy puppy dog!
Last change a bedroom light into a brave knight!
Abracadabra!

Jake and Mohamad

Making Magic

What to do

* From Meg and Mog to Winnie and Wilbur, young readers are very familiar with wizardry, wands and magic tricks. Here's an activity for them to create some tricks of their own.

* First, invite the children to imagine that they have their own magic wands. Like all wands, theirs can change one thing into something else. However, the really special thing about their wands is that the two things always **rhyme** with each other, as in Jake and Mohamad's work on page 95.

* Explain that they are going to write a sequence of **commands** for their wands to carry out, to show off their magical transforming powers.

* The curriculum for both English and maths at Key Stage 1 states explicitly that children should experience sequencing sentences in chronological order for short narratives or explanations.

* Therefore, to get their ideas into an order, they'll need some of these words and phrases to begin each command:

    Next   Then   First   After that   Last of all   Finally   Now   Later

* Show these and ask children to order them to make a proper sequence. Clearly, there isn't only one right answer, and some share a meaning, so offer children choices in their writing.

* After each first word or phrase, writers need a **verb** commanding the wand to work – *change*, *make* and *turn* are used in the piece on page 95. Other possibilities are *alter* and *transform*.

* As well as thinking of their own rhyming items, Jake and Mohamad used a simple rhyming dictionary to research in for further ideas. They were asked to add details to each pair of rhyming words to make the command that bit more vivid.

* Finally, once their commands are set down, writers need to add the **exclamation mark** to complete each one.

Differentiation suggestion

* The more able could be asked to come up with **alliterating adjectives** for each of the two nouns in every spell.

Full Colour

What is Pink?

What is pink? A rose is pink
by the fountain's brink.

What is red? A poppy's red
in its barley bed.

What is blue? The sky is blue
where the clouds float through.

What is white? A swan is white
sailing in the night.

What is yellow? Pears are yellow,
rich and ripe and mellow.

What is green? The grass is green,
with small flowers between.

What is violet? Clouds are violet
in the summer twilight.

What is orange? Why, an orange,
just an orange!

Christina Rossetti

Full Colour

What to do

* Christina Rossetti was born in London in 1830 and lived there all her life until her death in 1894. She was a lively little girl – her father called her and her brother the 'two storms'. She wrote poetry throughout her life, including many poems for children. 'What is Pink?' is one of the best known.

* Begin by reading Rossetti's poem together. Talk about the poem – the colours she includes and the things she chooses to exemplify each colour. Are there colours she hasn't included? Would the children have different examples for any of the colours? Do they agree with the last verse?

* Go on to discuss how each verse of the poem is made, with its repeated two-sentence pattern:

    * line 1: the opening question and colour. Then on the same line the chosen item and the colour repeated as the line's last word.

    * line 2: telling you more about that thing, a vivid and enjoyable detail. This makes the whole line an **expanded noun phrase**.

* Explain that the children are going to write their own poems in the style of 'What Is Pink?' For each new verse they write, they'll need a fresh colour and should then copy the form of the original poem – but without the rhyming. They should instead put their efforts every time into thinking of an object and a detail that brings it to life for their readers, as in this extract from Irene's poem:

    What is red? Traffic lights are red
    telling the cars and buses to stop.

    What is purple? A grape is purple
    safe inside my lunch box.

    What is black? The night is black
    everywhere outside my bedroom window.

* If your writers like Rossetti's last verse, then perhaps they can 'borrow' it as a final flourish to their own poems. This will mean that they have featured a **full stop**, **question mark** and **exclamation mark** in this one piece of writing.

As I Was Going to ...

As I was going to St. Ives,
I met a man with seven wives.
Each wife had seven sacks.
Each sack had seven cats.
Each cat had seven kits.
Kits, cats, sacks and wives –
How many were going to St Ives?

Anon

As I was going to Bridlington,
I met one mole that was digging two holes.
I met three snakes that were baking four cakes.
I met five goats that were wearing six coats.
I met seven bees that were stinging eight knees.
I met nine snails that were leaving ten trails.
How many were going to Bridlington?

Adam, Liam and Alex

As I Was Going to ...

What to do

* Whether you read the 18th century original or the 21st century re-write, the answer is the same – just one, as everyone and everything else was going the other way.

* That original still has real appeal and the ability to catch the unwary – and, as the boys' work shows, it is one well worth imitating.

* Start by enjoying the original rhyme together and tell the children they are going to write their own riddles in the same style.

* Writers begin with the shared first line, ending it with a destination of their choice.

* Next, they write *I met* five times down the page as line openings.

* Now they need to think of or research five animals – and then words to rhyme with each one.

* The three boys had a simple rhyming dictionary, which proved invaluable for both aspects.

* Show the children the repeated pattern of each two-clause sentence they must write – with its **conjunction** *that* and the **verb**, saying what the animal was doing – always in the **past progressive tense**.

* Explain the 1–10 sequence of the five lines, and how this adds to the comical nonsense of the whole.

* The final line rounds it all off with the **question**, returning to the form of the original.

Something to Shout About!

> Oh sparkle my sleep! – say it when you are tired
> Oh lift our legs! – for when you are excited
> Oh whisper my wellies! – this is for surprised
> Oh paint my parrot! – this means you are grumpy
>
> Group made collection

What to do

* **Exclamation marks** need exclamations to exclaim about. There are lots of one-word ones like *Ouch!* and *Wow!* but this activity gets a bit more inventive.

* In an episode of *The BFG*, Roald Dahl's giant takes Sophie dream-hunting; when he catches a particularly good dream, he gets very excited and exclaims, '*Oh swipe my swoggles!*' and '*Oh mince my maggots!*' and '*Oh save our solos!*'

* To begin, ask the children to suggest the different moods and feelings they have, such as happiness, fear, surprise, pain and so on. List their ideas for all to see. Explain that we use the exclamation mark when we write and want to show one of these strong moods or feelings.

* Share the BFG's three exclamations and discuss how each begins with the interjection *Oh* after which come two words, first a **verb**, then a **noun**; both words start with the same letter to make a memorable **alliterating phrase**. Joined with *my* or *our*, the exclamation is complete, needing only its closing punctuation.

* Ask writers now to compose their own exclamations in the same style as the BFG's. They can explore dictionaries for their pairs of words; the more unlikely the pairing of their words the better. Encourage also invented words as in the BFG's *swoggles*.

* When writers have their exclamations, have them look again at the list of moods and feelings made earlier. Ask them now to decide on the mood or feeling, which they think best suits each of their freshly composed exclamations.

* A group of more able children can now work to collect and edit all the class exclamations to produce their 'Class Guide to Exclaiming', like the example above. They should ensure that they have at least one exclamation for every mood identified in the opening session.

A Few of My Favourite Things

Cottage
When I live in a Cottage
I shall keep in my Cottage
    Two different Dogs
    Three creamy Cows
    Four giddy Goats
    Five pewter Pots
    Six silver Spoons
    Seven busy Beehives
    Eight ancient Appletrees
    Nine red Rosebushes
    Ten teeming Teapots
    Eleven chirping Chickens
    Twelve cosy Cats with their kittenish Kittens
        and
    One blessèd Baby in a Basket.
That's what I'll have when I live in my Cottage.
                            Eleanor Farjeon

Castle
When I live in a castle
I shall keep in my castle
    two park swings,
    three silver tiaras,
    four sparkly tops,
    five bright rainbows,
    six sweet fairy cakes
        and
    one pair of cosy pyjamas under my pillow.
That's what I'll have when I live in my castle.
                            Bess

A Few of My Favourite Things

What to do

✱   The first thing to do here is read Eleanor Farjeon's poem and explore all it has to offer. It's a great piece about choice and independence and it's also full of enjoyable (and accessible) details: the poet's pick of her perfect home; the things she wants to have with her; the increasing number of each item in her list right up to the final unexpected switch to just 'One'; the alliterating adjectives and nouns.

✱   The construction of the poem provides an excellent model for children's own writing. It offers them a supportive structure and at the same time challenges them to think of their own content.

✱   The starting point is to ask the writers to choose their own ideal home – palace, garage, flat, railway station, etc – and what they want inside. These things can be things they already own and love and also things they would like to have.

✱   How much of the original poem young writers then follow is very much a matter for individual teachers to decide. Bess, you can see, plans to move into a castle; she keeps the numbering sequence just up to six; she keeps the **adjective** + **noun** pattern but not the original's alliteration.

✱   It's worth pointing out to the class that most of what they write, with its expanded **noun phrases** and the separating **commas** in the ever growing list, will probably be the longest single **sentence** they have set down in their writing lives so far!

Differentiation suggestion

✱   More able children should be encouraged to model their pieces more exactly on the original poem: create 10 to 12 items in their 'home'; use alliterating adjective-noun phrases throughout; perhaps alliterating these phrases off each opening number – something Eleanor Farjeon didn't attempt!

All Creatures Great and Small

> **The Prayer of the Green Frog**
>
> Dear God,
> Can I have lots of water to keep my skin wet?
> Give me a safe pond to live in and lay my eggs.
> Let my eggs become tadpoles and then lots and lots of green frogs.
> Can I have a very sticky tongue to catch tasty bugs?
> Please give me a loud croak.
> Protect me from the pesky heron that wants to catch me and eat me.
>
> Isabel

What to do

* The inspiration for this activity (and Isabel's poem) comes from two sources you won't often see put together: the KS1 science orders and a Benedictine Abbey in France. A nun in the abbey, Carmen Bernos de Gasztold, wrote some poems, which she called Prayers from the Ark. Years later, the poems were found in a cupboard in the abbey, published, translated into English and have been popular ever since. Each poem is in the form of a prayer, spoken by a particular animal. In each case, the poet bases the prayer on the creature's needs and fears, as well as giving each a distinctive and recognisable character.

* Now to the science orders. The curriculum for KS1 asks that children study animals: the habitats and micro-habitats to which they are suited; their production of offspring; their place in a simple food chain; their predators, if any.

* In the example above, Isabel first read and listened to a selection of the original poems and then used biological features in turn to create the individual lines for her frog's prayer.

* Examples of the original prayer-poems are readily available online. As well as providing delightful pieces in themselves, they will also provide writers with the model for their own writing. A particular focus should be on the way requests in prayers begin, as you can see in Isabel's poem.

* A final task is for writers to check their written ideas to see if each is a question needing a question mark, or a request needing a full stop.

* The guidance to the science curriculum wants children to communicate their ideas and understanding 'in a variety of ways'. Animals offering prayers certainly makes its contribution to that variety.

This Hand

This Hand

throws a ball in the playground,

holds my guinea pigs Bubble and Squeak,

paints pictures of castles,

puts spaghetti into my mouth,

waves to the man in the moon at bedtime.

Jimmy

This Hand

What to do

* To begin this activity, simply collect and display all the things the children can suggest that they can do with their hands. There's no need to include details, just the root **verbs** at this stage.

* Tell the children that they are going to write short poems describing what their own hands can do. The opening line – and also the poem's title – is 'This Hand'. Below this they must now write five verbs. They might choose verbs from the class collection and/or ideas of their own. However, they need to choose verbs showing five different activities, to suggest the range of things a hand does. And they must remember to add the **suffix** -s/-es to each verb.

* Ask the writers to expand each line by adding descriptive details after each of their verbs, in the manner of Jimmy's example on page 105.

* When the writers have their five lines, they are ready for the second part of the task. For this, they need a clean piece of plain paper. They put one of their hands sideways onto the paper, spread their fingers and draw around the outline. A good tip is to turn the paper so that the finger ends are to the left. This will ensure that children are always writing into open space for the remainder of the task below.

* Children write the title above the outline and rewrite their five lines, one line inside each of the four fingers and thumb. This makes a good handwriting task, as children write to fit each line neatly inside each finger.

* What they have now is a shape-poem with the five lines representing the bones inside each finger. The poem is one long sentence, needing one **capital letter** and one **full stop** – with a separating **comma** at the end of each line.

* It might help to show the class X-ray images of a hand (readily available on the internet) to make clear to the children just what they have created.

* It might also be a good time to introduce children to the wonderful world of shape poems – from Guillaume Apollinaire at the start of the 20th century to Gina Douthwaite today.

On Your Marks

It is frogspawn in a pond.
    It is an eyeball looking at you.
     It is a full stop.

It is a black cat's tail,
    a whistle for football,
    a comma.

Is it a pirate's hook?
    Is it a long upside down sock?
    Is it a question mark?

It is Winnie the Witch's wand!
    It is a rocket going into space!
    It is an exclamation mark!

Group made poem

On Your Marks

What to do

* During their Key Stage 1 years, children are expected to learn to use and understand the purpose of four bits of **punctuation**: **full stops**, **commas**, **question marks** and **exclamation marks**.

* This activity invites children to look long and hard at each of those four marks and imagine what other things there are that look similar to them.

* The obvious starting point is to have children study each item of punctuation and come up with their suggestions. That is how the group-made piece on page 107 began, followed by discussion of which two of all the suggestions should be kept in the actual poem, with the item of punctuation coming in the final line.

* A further development is then to write each verse of the poem using punctuation that matches the subject.

* So, verse 1 is in three sentences ending in full stops; verse 2 is a list with items separated by commas; verse 3 asks questions; and verse 4 gets good and excited!

* The Key Stage 1 syllabus for mathematics features its own signs and symbols and some of these can readily be included in the activity.

* Posters featuring all the ideas – especially those not being included in the poems – make enjoyable and useful classroom displays.

Chain Whispers

What to do

∗ Sometimes called Chinese Whispers and even, it seems, Russian Gossip! Strange, as it's a game with its origins in Victorian England, and still played and enjoyed to this day.

∗ Players sit in a circle and one player whispers a message to the next player, who passes it on to the next player and so on round. Inevitably the original message gets much mangled in its whispered transmissions and the fun lies in hearing all the changes and seeing where they occurred.

∗ For a classroom version of the game, here is a traditional children's rhyme:

> 'Have you got a sister?
> he south wind kissed her!
>
> Have you got a brother?
> He's made of purple rubber!
>
> Have you got a baby?
> It's made of bread and gravy!

∗ With the players in a circle, whisper the rhyme's first line to player 1, who then whispers it to player 2 and so on round all the chain. Whispering finished, now listen to each player's version in turn. Finally show everyone the original rhyme's second line, comparing it with your own.

∗ Start to write a class version of the rhyme, using the original's first line and your players' final or favourite 'whisper'. Repeat the game using the second and third questions. After each round, add these original lines, plus your own two new lines to your class version.

∗ Show the whole original rhyme and draw pupils' attention to the **question marks**, **exclamation marks** and **speech marks** (if you wish) and explain their different purposes.

∗ Your new second lines might be statements or questions, so involve the children in deciding and adding the correct bits of punctuation to your class version.

∗ Whoever wrote that original rhyme, probably did so by playing the game inside their own heads to get to their own mangled final version. Confident writers can be asked to work in the same way. You might provide them with some opening questions which avoid the whispered messages becoming predictable. So maybe, 'Have you met a polar bear?' or 'Have you ever had chicken pox?' A rhyming dictionary can obviously be useful here.

Note: Chain Whispers works best when played with a large group so there are lots of possibilities for changes. However, taking turns, with half the class playing and half watching the developing 'experiment', also works well.

Oh, Do Be So Silly!

An apostrophe
won't sing a pop song to you,
can't fly into space on its own,
doesn't have porridge for breakfast,
mustn't take my pencil from me,
hasn't got any arms or legs,
isn't good to eat.

                Mae

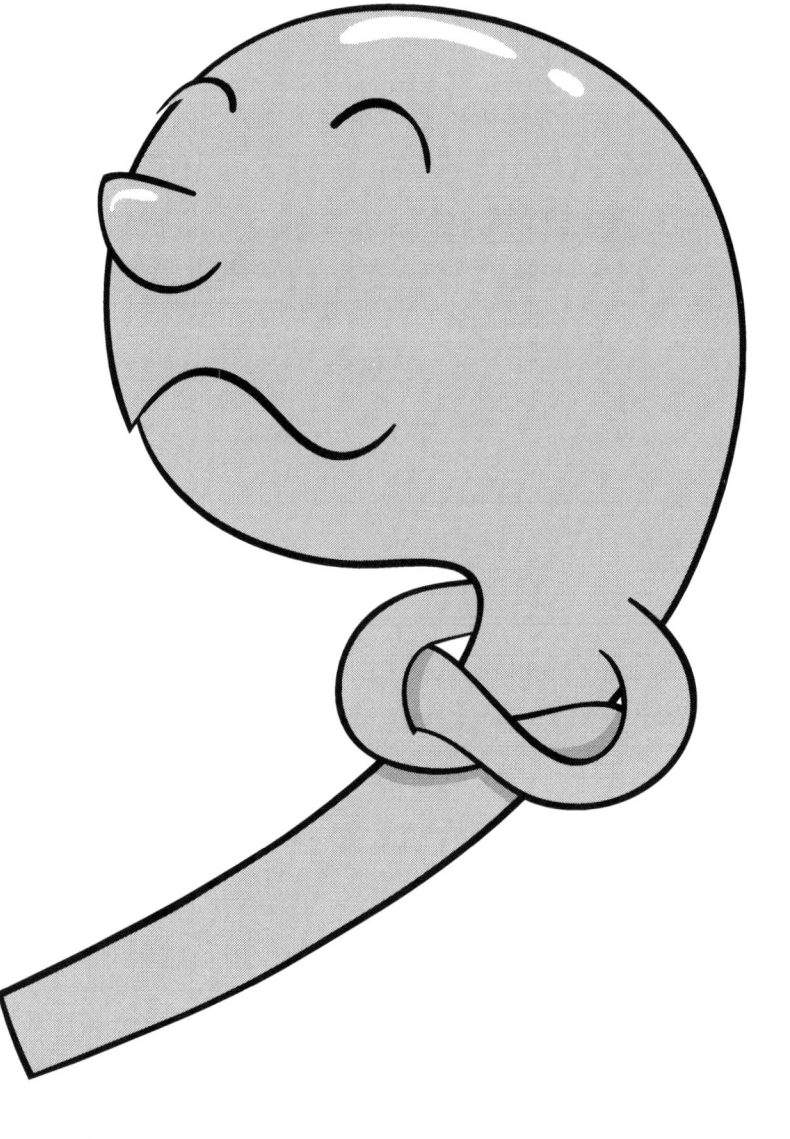

Oh, Do Be So Silly!

What to do

✽ Of all the items of punctuation, the **apostrophe** must be the most troublesome. First, it has two totally different functions:

  ✦ to mark ownership

  ✦ to indicate where letters are missing in verbal contractions.

✽ In neither function is there complete clarity. So, for example, we shop in Sainsbury's and also in Boots; we once bought books in Waterstone's but now we go to Waterstones. In contractions, we have an apostrophe to show the lost 'o' in 'isn't' but there's no apostrophe to show the lost double 'll' when 'shall not' becomes 'shan't'.

✽ Muddled and confusing as all this is, the apostrophe doesn't seem to be going away and Key Stage 1 children have to encounter it. However, if they have to take it seriously, that doesn't mean they can't also have some fun with it. Here's a way they might do both.

✽ The focus is on the apostrophe's use to mark missing letters, specifically the omitted 'o' when 'not' is shortened and attached to verbs such as these:

  does   can*   will*   must   should   is   has   could   would

✽ These are sometimes called 'helping verbs' as they usually appear before another main verb to help it change its normal meaning – as in Mae's poem on page 115. They are fully introduced to children in Key Stage 2. They are useful here, precisely because in their shortened negative form, they always have the apostrophe in the same place, marking the omitted 'o'.

✽ If necessary, introduce the subject by showing the children the verbs above plus the word 'not', making two separate words each time. Then show the children how the contracted form is made every time and tell them they are now going to use these contractions to write some very silly lines to make an extremely silly poem.

✽ Writers begin, like Mae, by writing *An apostrophe*. Below that, down the page, they list the contractions with their apostrophes in any order they choose.

✽ Once all the contractions are in place, they complete each line by adding the silliest thing that an apostrophe *can't/doesn't/mustn't* do. Less confident writers than Mae can be asked to complete each line with just the verb – but it must be a different verb each time.

✽ When writers have their lines, they need to see that their poems are a single sentence, needing one **capital letter** and one **full stop**; each line should end with a **comma**; finally, of course, they must be sure they have an **apostrophe** in its correct space every time.

These words are exceptions. In 'can't', the second 'n' is omitted as well as the 'o'. 'Will not' changes to 'won't'.

I am a Who - Not a What

> I am Phoebe McAuliffe.
>   I'm not a pink monkey.
>   I'm not a plain map.
>   I'm not a perfect mummy.
>   I'm not a purple monster.
>   I'm not a playful mouse.
> I am Phoebe McAuliffe.

What to do

* No prizes for guessing what's going on here! Phoebe was asked to write down who she is and then use the initials of her first and last names to say some of the things she is not.

* Each line begins with *I'm not*, followed by an **adjective** and a **noun**, beginning with the letters appropriate to the writer. It's also a chance to introduce the I am **contraction** *I'm* with its **apostrophe** for the missing letter.

* A way to start, and to show at once the playful nature of the activity, is to have an adult say who they are and then add a number of things that they are not.

* If the adult modelling the activity also uses a dictionary to search for their adjectives and nouns, this all helps encourage children to see the dictionary as a rich treasury and research tool, not just a means for checking spellings. And of course, children can have access to a dictionary, and join in to suggest words for the adult.

* As well as simply thinking of their adjectives and nouns, children should then be encouraged to explore dictionaries on a word-hunt of their own. Locating letters even in picture dictionaries will provide fresh and entertaining objects/nouns. Talking and thinking about suitable adjectives helps them see the real differences word choices make.

* Those with middle or multiple names could extend their 'what nots' with extra adjectives – and possibly adverbs.

* Finally, the activity can be extended by children writing similar pieces for Mother's Day and Father's Day.

Simply Super!

When Isla's superclever she'll get every hard sum right.

When Ellie's superstretchy she'll be the best goalkeeper for Wales.

When my big brother's supernaughty he'll play Minecraft all day.

When my baby brother's supernoisy he'll make us all deaf.

When Mrs Aldcroft's supersmall she'll live in my dolls house.

When I'm superinvisible I'll dip my finger into the chocolate pudding in the fridge.

Mariam

Simply Super!

What to do

* Of all the **prefixes**, *super-* has to be the most used. It is also the one most readily recognised by children – *Superman*, *superstar*, *supermarket*, and so on.

* You can add *super-* to almost any root word to make it more, better or greater. This activity uses **adjectives** throughout, as Mariam's piece shows. Also, it offers a playful introduction to the use of **apostrophes** to show where letters are missing.

* Begin by collecting – or displaying – a number of features, qualities, moods we all have or would like to have. For example, as well as the ones in Mariam's piece, you might get:

fast	hungry	good	inventive	tiny
strong	kind	tall	friendly	sleepy	cool

* Use any of your **adjectives** to talk together, discussing how we might show we are *strong*, and then how we might be if we become *superstrong*.

* For their writing, children must now choose any of their friends and family and give to each one a particular superpower. Each power can only be given once.

* Show the writers the pattern of each sentence they will be writing:

    + start with *When,*
    + add the chosen person's name or relationship – with the necessary *'s*
    + next the **adjective** plus its *super-* prefix
    + and then the correct **pronoun** - with the necessary *'ll*
    + finally, what the person will do with the power, as in the lines above. The more imaginative, the better!

* When everybody has written their first line, this might be a good time to check on SPaG issues – as well as inventiveness.

* Writers now go on to award superpowers, using their first line as a model.

* Finally, each writer can give themselves a superpower, making this the closing line of their piece. Super duper!

Two Little Words

I can ride my bike but I can't yet reach the high shelf.

I can climb a tree but I can't yet turn on the kettle.

I can use a screwdriver but I can't yet read a book myself.

I can walk two and a half miles but I can't yet crack an egg.

I can eat lots of peas but I can't yet drink beer.

Eddie

Two Little Words

What to do

* Young children often think that long words are better than short words, and that growing up will be all about learning ever longer words. This is not surprising because we adults are always aiming 'long words' in their direction. And yet the truth is that short words carry the real power – nowhere more so than *Yes* and *No*.

* In Eddie's piece, for all the enjoyable details, the key words in his meanings are *but* and *yet*.

* Children are generally comfortable with the **conjunction** *and*, used to join two simple sentences together to make one compound one. *And* just adds information, as in *I have a sister **and** I have a brother*. The conjunction *but*, however, is a lot more fun because it sets up a contrast, as in *I like sunshine **but** I don't like rain*.

* In Eddie's piece, the second short word *yet*, is crucial because it means 'up until now' and therefore strongly implies that the things he can't do now, he will be able to do in the future.

* To begin the work, discuss together the things your children can do now.

* Next, move on to considering the things they can't quite do; the things they are learning to do; the things they are looking forward to being able to do in the future.

* Ask children to make two lists: things they *can do* and things they *can't yet do*.

* Show and explain the form of the compound sentence, *I can … but I can't yet ….* Ask them to put their two lists together with one item from each list in each **compound sentence**, being sure to include *but* and *yet* in each one.

* Finally, use the opportunity to point out the need for the **apostrophe** in *can't* to show that two words have been squashed together to make one word with letters missing.

The Caretaker's Crocodile

The caretaker's crocodile is an upset crocodile and her name is Ursula.
The caretaker's crocodile is a valuable crocodile and her name is Violet.
The caretaker's crocodile is a warm crocodile and his name is William.
The caretaker's crocodile is an exciting crocodile and his name is Exit.
The caretaker's crocodile is a yellow crocodile and her name is Yolande.
The caretaker's crocodile is a zippy crocodile and his name is Zayn.

Extract from class made piece

The Caretaker's Crocodile

What to do

* In Victorian times, this was a popular parlour game known usually as The Minister's Cat.

* However, as a classroom activity, it gets the verbal fun started right away by choosing an adult known to the children and giving them a pet – as unusual as you like so long as it alliterates! Perhaps *The Headteacher's Hippo* or *The Dinner Ladies' Dragon*.

* Once owner and pet are agreed, write up the title, and below, the same words as a sentence opening. Explain that the aim is to write a whole A-Z for the creature. For each letter of the alphabet you're going to need one word to describe the pet (an **adjective**) and a name. Like this, starting with A:

    The caretaker's crocodile is an a_____ crocodile and her/his name is A_____

* The letter *x* is problematic so, as you can see in the extract on page 117, the class used *ex* to make the adjective's letter-sound and made up a name from a matching noun.

* Once the children understand the pattern, you can go on working all together, or ask pairs or individual children to go off to work on particular lines and letters. Whatever the approach, this is a good opportunity to introduce dictionary research to young writers. Show how dictionaries mark adjectives and encourage children to look for and consider a few before choosing one. This gets them used to seeing the dictionary as a 'treasure chest' in Sandy Brownjohn's phrase, and not merely a device for checking spellings.

* Names for the pet won't be in a dictionary, so this needs some real-life research: see who can suggest names for trickier letters and as an enjoyable homework task, ask children to bring in useful family first names – grandparents being a particularly valuable source!

* As well as vocabulary development, there is a lot of necessary SPaG material squeezed in here: punctuating sentences; using an **apostrophe** to mark singular **possession**; **possessive adjectives** (*her, his*); **capital letters** for names; using the **conjunction** *and* to join two clauses.

A First Abecedarius

A was an apple pie.
B bit it.
C cut it.
D dealt it.
E eat it.
F fought for it.
G got it.
H had it.
I inspected it.
J joined for it.
K kept it.
L longed for it.
M mourned for it.
N nodded at it.
O opened it.
P peeped at it.
Q quartered it.
R ran for it.
S stole it.
T took it.
U upset it.
V viewed it.
W wanted it.
X, Y, Z and **&**

all wished for a piece in hand.

A First Abecedarius

What to do

* The poem on page 120 may very well be the very first English abecedarius – or ABC Book – having been around for 400 years or so, teaching countless generations of children their alphabetical order.

* To begin, read the whole through together. You might even try covering up some of the **alliterating verbs** to see if they can guess them. Explain also that the funny squiggle at the end of the penultimate line is called an **ampersand** and means simply *and*.

* The English language has evolved since the piece was first published in the 18th century, and so one of the verbs jars at once: *eat*, which must now, of course, be *ate*. See if the children can spot it. Can they suggest a different verb, which would be correct?

* Tell the children they are going to make their own abecedarius. The maker of that first abecedarius chose 'A' to be *an apple pie*. Today, we might choose an *acrobat, aeroplane, adventure* among others. However, for language purposes, the best opening might just be:

    A was the alphabet.

* Offer that first line and invite suggestions for verbs for each subsequent letter. Any verb works, so for example:

    B bounced on it.
    C cuddled it.

* This can be an activity for a whole class; alternatively, pairs or individuals can be given a letter to research in a dictionary and then contribute their choice to the whole. Be sure you ask children look for *x* verbs under *ex*.

* Point out to the children the use of **capital** and **lower-case letters** in the original and ask that they follow the same pattern.

* Each letter-line can go on to make one page of a brand new full-colour illustrated abecedarius, to add to a great unbroken tradition.

Differentiation suggestion

* More able children can be further tasked with providing alliterating **adverbs** to add to each line.

Note: The original text is written in the **past tense**, though it also works perfectly well in the **present tense**. Whichever tense you choose, you'll be helping pupils to develop consistent use of verb tense throughout their piece.

The Animals Do Fancy Dress

a dog with a zebra's stripes
a goldfish with a peacock's tail
a snake with a rabbit's ears
a cat with a bird's feathers
an elephant with a polar bear's fur
a shark with a robin's red breast

Finn

The Animals Do Fancy Dress

What to do

* Everyone likes dressing up – young children most of all. But what if the animals could join in? That's the idea behind this activity.

* Children write as many short lines as they can, each featuring one animal 'wearing' some detail from another.

* The pattern of each line is the same throughout; these lines are **phrases** not full sentences, so no need for capital letters and full stops.

* This means that as well as coming up with some great 'outfits', writers can focus all their punctuation-related attention to the need for an **apostrophe** in each line, used here to mark singular possession in nouns.

* Make it clear that every line starts with one animal, which then comes to the party dressed up with a detail taken from one other, different animal.

Differentiation suggestions

* More confident writers can be asked to have two items of fancy dress. These need to be enjoyably different from each other and joined together with *and* to create a **compound phrase**. For example:

   a penguin with a hedgehog's prickles and a robin's red breast

* Completed lines might then be presented as captions to cartoon drawings or larger scale artwork – possibly all done with Camille Saint-Saëns' 'Carnival of the Animals' playing inspirationally in the background.

Adventures with Adverbs

Quietly

Quietly the fox stalks its prey.
Quietly the cat sleeps in the hay.
Quietly the man sits in his chair.
Quietly the mermaid combs her hair.

Quietly the swan glides down the river.
Quietly the snake begins to slither.
Quietly moves the moon – but most quiet of all
Is the thinking I've done watching leaves fall.

Aenaone Tickler

Cleverly

Cleverly Govinda says things in Hindi.
Cleverly spiders make webs every day.
Cleverly leopards run so fast and don't stop to drink.
Cleverly my bedroom lamp goes on and off when I touch it.
But cleverest is me when I spell the word because.

Tyler

Adventures with Adverbs

What to do

✻ 'Quietly' might not be great literature, but it's ideal – and also calming – for children to read, study and use as a model for their own creative writing.

✻ Very helpfully, Aenaone Tickler has the **adverb** *quietly* as both her title and the opening word of each line of her poem, before converting it into an **adjective** in her final line.

✻ Children readily grasp what adverbs do in a sentence – they 'add' something to the **verb**, and in this case the adverb tells the reader how something is being done.

✻ Read the poem all together, focusing attention on that repeated adverb and the concluding adjective. What more quiet things can the children suggest that the poet doesn't include? Write their ideas up, beginning *Quietly* each time to show and reinforce the learning of the lines' structure.

✻ Most adverbs are formed by adding the **suffix** *-ly* to the root adjective, and helpfully again, Ms. Tickler has used an adjective only needing the suffix and no other spelling changes. Here are some more adjectives also needing no modification:

> loud   quick   silent   wild   excited   soft   slow

✻ Ask pupils to use one chosen adjective to write their own poems in the style of 'Quietly'. Once they have their adjective, they should begin by writing it down with an opening capital letter and adverbial suffix. They must then complete the line with an idea that suits their adverb's meaning as Tyler did with his poem 'Cleverly'.

✻ Writers shouldn't try to rhyme their lines but should rather aim for a range and variety of ideas in their lines.

✻ Finally, and as in the original poem, writers compose a closing line using their adjective as an adjective – with either *most* before it or the suffix *-est* added, this time showing how the word applies to them.

Differentiation suggestion

✻ Instead of a single verse poem, more able writers might write two verses using root adjectives with opposite meanings (**antonyms**) such as *soft/loud* or *quick/slow*.

Silly Suffixes

There were three ghosts
sitting on posts
eating buttered toasts
and greasing their fists
right up to their wrists.
Weren't they beasts
to make such feasts!

There were three ghostesses
sitting on postesses
eating buttered toastesses
and greasing their fistesses
right up to their wristesses.
Weren't they beastesses
to make such feastesses!

Silly Suffixes

What to do

* The National Curriculum for English is very keen on **suffixes** and wants them introduced in Year 1 and added to children's working terminology in Year 2. This activity aims to put some fun into the matter, starting with the old rhyme on page 125. You can share both versions with the children, asking them first which one they think is the published version, the one to be found in books. The answer is the second one – a silly tale, made even sillier with the addition of those extra bits at the end of each line.

* Those bits are suffixes. Spend any time you need exploring and explaining what suffixes are and what they do: letters added to the end of a word to make a new word or change the job a word is doing. For example, *cat/s*; *sing/er*; *enjoy/ment*.

* Now point out that the suffix *–esses* in that rhyme doesn't do either of those things. Its job is to make something silly even sillier!

* Time now to find more old rhymes and try the same trick. You can work all together on one rhyme, or have children working on different rhymes to see what fun might be had.

* Have a selection of common suffixes ready to display for the children to work with. These can be a single letter, like the pluralising *-s*, or two letters such as *-er*, *-es*, and *-ly* that turns adjectives into adverbs; or three letters, like *-ing* and *-ful*; or four letters like *-less*, *-ment* or *-ness*. Differentiation can be achieved by ensuring that children work with a suffix they are currently learning to use elsewhere in their literacy work.

* You can keep the same suffix for all the line-ends, as here:

    Handy Pandy, Jack-a-dandyly,
    loves plum cake and sugar candyly.
    He bought some at the grocer's shoply
    and out he came, hop, hop, hoply!

* Finally, your eagle-eyed children might spot that the original rhyme uses two suffixes to make its nonsense: *-ess* (as in *lion/ess*) plus the plural *-es*. Perhaps they can try the same trick, as here:

    Little Jack Hornermenter
    sat in a cornermenter,
    eating his Christmas piementer.
    He put in his thumbmenter
    and pulled out a plummenter
    and said, What a good boy am Imenter!

* During and after the writing, shared readings of the silliness is, of course, essential.

Three of a Kind

White is a sheep.
Whiter is my paper.
Whitest is a polar bear.

    Green is a leaf on a tree.
    Greener is a crossing light.
    Greenest is the Hungry Caterpillar.

        Yellow is the sun.
        Yellower is a bowl of custard.
        Yellowest is Homer Simpson.

            Nell

Three of a Kind

What to do

* As with many SPaG issues, there is no requirement that children in Key Stage 1 learn the terms **comparative** and **superlative** in relation to **adjectives**. However, they do need to encounter the **suffixes** -er and -est as the ways adjectives modify their meanings.

* Adjectives defining colours are useful here, first because of children's strong responses to colours, and second because most of the most common ones need little or no spelling adjustments beyond the addition of the suffixes.

* Start the activity by offering a good selection of colour adjectives. For example:

    red   white   brown   blue   black   green   yellow   grey   pink

* The children must choose and note down three different colours. Then, they note down three things that are each of their chosen colours. Emphasise the need for variety here, by choosing three different things. So maybe not *snow, snowball, snowman* under *white*.

* Next, they write the three forms of each adjective – plus *is* – one under the other. If anyone has chosen *red*, they will need to double the final consonant to make *redder* and *reddest*. For *white* and *blue*, writers just need to add *-r* and *-st*, because the *e* is already in place.

* Writers now complete each line in turn by choosing which of their things they think has the least of the colour; which has more of the colour; and finally, which one has most of the colour.

* Emphasise throughout that there are no right or wrong choices. It is always a matter of personal reaction and always interesting to see the different ideas different people have.

Haiku for Beginners

Happy is playing with daddy.
Happier is the wind blowing round me.
Happiest is going on holiday.

        Francesca

Cold is a penguin's belly.
Colder is the Antarctic in the winter.
Coldest is the Mersey water.

        Jordan

Haiku for Beginners

What to do

* The tiny Japanese poem, the haiku, seems to get everywhere – even sometimes forming clues on BBC 1's quiz show, Pointless.

* English versions of the haiku usually keep just three features of the original. They are written in three lines; the lines have 5, 7 and 5 syllables respectively; there's no rhyme.

* The haikus by Francesca and Jordan observe two of those features, but rather than being counted in syllables, their lines have 5, 7, 5 words.

* Here's a haiku to help writers always remember the pattern, whether in syllables or words:

    My first line has five,
    and my middle line must have seven.
    Then five to end me.

* The three short lines of the haiku make it just right for exploring the way **adjectives** add **suffixes** (-*er*, -*est*) to the root word to make their **comparative** and **superlative** forms.

* Here are some adjectives your children might choose from:

    short   slow   quick   high   old   hot   long   dark

* You could include some adjectives with trickier spellings – like happy (used in Francesca's poem on page 129), big/bigger, late/later.

* The three forms of each chosen adjective form the openings to the haiku's lines, followed by *is*. The writers then complete the lines as they wish.

Differentiation suggestions

* Encourage confident writers to experiment with saying each idea for a line in different ways to help them get just the right word total.

* For less sure writers, using and spelling the three adjectival forms might be their real achievement – and haiku which don't conform exactly to the 5-7-5 pattern are just an acceptable new variant.

Happy Endings

You drink out of this **ss**.
This **ss** is all of us in this room.

My rabbit lives in this **tch**.
This **tch** has a black cat and rides a broom.

I am this **ful** when I don't remember.
It was this **ful** when I banged my head.

This **ness** is the night.
When we have this **ness** we stay off school.

                    Selected from class-made collections

glass; class; hutch, witch; forgetful, painful; darkness, illness (or sickness)

Happy Endings

What to do

* Small, one-line riddles like those can work for both **spelling pattern** word-endings and also **suffixes**.

* Start by choosing the word-ending(s) you want to focus on. To introduce the activity, it might help to make up some one-liners of your own to try out on the children.

* Have a larger selection of words ready to share and add to, in order to explore together how the one-sentence clues work. One point to make is that the answer-word mustn't be included in the riddle! Make up different riddles for a word to see which works best.

* Ask the children now to make up their own riddles, using the endings and suffixes you give them.

Differentiation suggestion

* If separate groups or classes work on different endings and suffixes, then riddles can be properly road-tested in swapping and sharing sessions. Differentiation can be achieved here by ensuring that children work with a suffix they are currently learning to use elsewhere in their literacy work.

Note: definitions of words in dictionaries can often be useful in helping riddlers create their clues.

Two's Company

Half of me you spread on toast.
Half of me holds a tiny drink.
All of me is a yellow flower.

                Jasmine and Bethan

I start as water coming from a cloud.
I end as a thing that shoots an arrow.
I make seven colours in the sky.

                Nathan and Isaac

My first half has five toes.
My second half is a sphere.
You score goals with me.

                Siobhan and Samira

buttercup; rainbow; football

Two's Company

What to do

* Compounding is a clever way we use ready-made bits of the language to make something new. Here it's **compound nouns** and in this activity, they are presented in the form of short riddles – the solutions to the ones on page 133 being *buttercup*, *rainbow* and *football*.

* Compound nouns are most often made by joining noun to noun as in those three examples. Sometimes it's an **adjective** joined to a **noun**, as in *whiteboard* and *Superman*.

* Here are some more examples, useful for making riddles:

    bedroom   goalpost   armchair   pancake   eyelid   bluebell   firework

    breakfast   daydream   thunderstorm   scarecrow   greenhouse

* Start by putting up a few compound nouns and ask the children what they notice about them. It won't be long before they spot that each word is made of two words.

* Choose one noun to work on together and explain that you are going to be making up some riddles. Each riddle will be just three short lines and it will be written as if the noun is speaking for itself.

* Each time the compound will describe itself: in line 1 with the first word in the compound; in line 2 with the second word; finally, as the complete compound.

* Offer introductions to the lines, like the examples on page 133, and encourage writers to come up with clues that just give the right balance of information and intrigue. Definitions in a dictionary can be helpful here.

* Once writers have their riddles, the final task is to give the solutions – at the bottom of the page and upside down, of course.

Spot the Difference

> What's the difference between ...?
>
> Straight away, you know there's a riddle coming! So, here is one:
>
> What's the difference between a giant and a gnome?
>
> And the answer is – the letter *g*, sounded in *giant*, silent in *gnome*.

What to do

* 'English Appendix 1: Spelling' specifies three **silent letter** issues for attention: *gn*, *kn* and *wr*. Always at the beginning of words, their examples include *gnat*, *knock*, *write*.

* Begin by collecting and sharing together more such words. Be sure to check what the dictionary has to offer.

* Next, introduce the idea of writing riddles featuring some of these words plus words where the same first letter is sounded, as in the example above. Here are a couple more to get things started:

    What's the difference between a knight and a kitten?
    What's the difference between wobbling and wriggling?

* Once the form of the riddle is clear to them, children can begin devising their own silent letter riddles. Encourage them first to think of or find pairs of words with that key difference of sound. The writing of the actual riddle is straightforward because of its repeated pattern.

Differentiation suggestions

* It is easier for less confident writers if the silent letter comes first or early in the word, as in the examples above. However, some children will enjoy exploring words where the silent letter is elsewhere, as this *b* at the end:

    What's the difference between a brush and a comb?

* Or this *t* the middle:

    What's the difference between listening and talking?

* Some children might also rise to the challenge of devising riddles where the two words are connected in some way as in the last two examples.

Note: don't miss the opportunity to point out that, as well as the creative fun, writers need to have a **capital letter**, **apostrophe** and **question mark** in every finished riddle.

Shape Riddles

> This sphere you can throw in winter.
> This sphere shines at night.
> This sphere is a fruit with a hard skin.
> And this sphere is an animal with prickles when it curls up.
>
> Eleanor

What to do

* By the end of Key Stage 1 children should be able to recognise and describe seven different 2D and 3D shapes. This riddle-writing idea seeks to do some of this work by having children think imaginatively about a geometric shape – as it appears in objects in the world around them.

* Start all together and choose one geometric shape to work on. What you do now will model the writing for the children, showing them the different steps in the process.

* Collect and list all the suggestions you get for objects that are the chosen shape.

* Explain that they are going to be writing riddles – shape riddles – so now they should choose items from the class list to make riddles for. Ask the children for suggestions, making it clear that you need objects that are quite different from one another. So, not just round fruits for a sphere, for example.

* When you have your objects, it's time to make up a one-sentence riddle for each one. The riddle has to be a clue, a short description of the object. Encourage ideas that might tease and puzzle a reader – not too hard and not too easy. And clues must not include the name of the object!

* When the children go off to compose their own riddles, remind them to repeat the stages in the writing they have just done together with you: first they choose a shape; next they make a list of objects that are that shape; then they choose some for riddles. Also point out the repeated line-openings to the riddles, allowing them to concentrate on the actual clues.

* Once the children have their riddles, it's time to test them out on one another.

* When the children come to make final drafts of their work, they do love writing the answers at the foot of their page – upside down of course!

* A classroom display of riddles featuring all seven geometric shapes would be a great outcome.

Writing Recipes

A Recipe to Make Playtime

1/2 bag of sunshine
67 carrier bags of friends
5 bottles of chasing
1 box of Mrs Spalton
3/4 kettle of wall games
22 pots of bumps and bangs
1/4 plate of whistle

Georgie and Callum

Writing Recipes

What to do

* The form of the recipe can be put to any purpose – except, in this activity, making something to eat.

* The recipe on page 137 is for a playtime, but you could also try recipes to make a season, a classroom, a festival, the seaside, a snowman. Or one to make the topic the children are working on at the moment. The possibilities are pretty much limitless.

* Start by asking the children to help you compile a list of the containers they can think of – from egg cups to swimming pools – and everything in between.

* Once a subject for the recipes is settled, ask the children, perhaps in small groups, to note down everything they can think of that belongs to the subject. These items will become the recipe's ingredients. Georgie and Callum's class took clipboards outside at playtime to carry out some real research and report back afterwards.

* Writers now need a page divided vertically into four columns, at the top of which they write the title of their recipe.

* They now work across the columns, putting in:

  + Column 1, a number. You can build in some differentiation here by tasking particular children with using numbers they are currently working on with you, for example fractions

  + Column 2, one of the containers from the class collection

  + Column 3, the word *of*

  + Column 4, any one of their ingredients.

Note: Writers can be encouraged to sprinkle tasty adjectives before some of their noun-ingredients. This activity can also be a useful one for looking at the times when writers need to add the suffix -*s* to make their nouns plural.

Who am I?

I have four legs.

I am very big.

I have thick, grey, wrinkly skin.

I have huge ears.

I live in Africa and India.

I have two white tusks and a long trunk.

Madeleine

Who am I?

What to do

* The theme here is animals, and the activity is a good route into drafting and sequencing writing.

* Explain to the children that they are going to be creating riddles – each one about a particular animal. Each riddle will give lots of clues for readers to guess an animal's identity.

* Begin by working as a class together and choose an animal to work on.

* Ask the children to say anything they know about this animal. Write each suggestion on a strip of card and display them for everyone to see.

* Remind the children that they are making riddles – so they don't want to give the answer too easily to a reader. Show them Madeleine's example on page 139 to let them see how she sequenced her ideas. What would have happened if she'd had her last line first?

* Ask the children now to sequence their ideas about their chosen animal by ordering the strips of information downwards, giving away as little as possible each time. Play around with the order until everyone is satisfied. This is active drafting!

* Finally, turn each idea into a statement, starting with *I*, imagining the animal is speaking for itself.

* Ask the children now to choose their own animal – one they know lots about – and work in just the same way on their own as they did when all together. The children should aim to have as many facts as possible, at least half a dozen, to make their riddles interesting as well as challenging.

Differentiation suggestion

* Less confident writers will benefit from having strips of paper to write their ideas on which they can then shuffle into a final order, as in the opening activity. More independent writers can list their ideas onto a page, and then number them to make the order, from most obscure to obvious.

Now We Are Six

When I was one,
I had just begun.

When I was two,
I was nearly new.

When I was three,
I was hardly me.

When I was four,
I was not much more.

When I was five,
I was just alive.

But now I am six,
I'm as clever as clever.

So I think I'll be six now
for ever and ever.

              A.A. Milne

When I was a baby, I slept in a cot.
When I was one, I crawled all day.
When I was two, I could walk and talk.
When I was three, I had teeth.
When I was four, I could eat grown up food.
When I was five, I could write my name.
But now I am six and a half, I have a bigger bike.

              Aaron

Now We Are Six

What to do

✱ Now almost 100 years old, A. A. Milne's poem 'Now We Are Six' is still popular and well worth sharing with Key Stage 1 children – who are, after all, exactly the poem's demographic.

✱ The children will thoroughly enjoy all the clever rhymes, but after that you have an opportunity to look a bit more critically: it's very short on details, isn't it? The poem doesn't say what it is really like to go through those different ages and stages. And no child wants to be six for ever, certainly not Aaron!

✱ The beginnings to the poem's seven lines are clearly set by Milne's original and your writers will now need to complete each line with a detail that is true for them. A good approach is to do some preparatory science work, looking at growth and development. Asking parents is obviously a useful homework assignment.

✱ The repeated pattern of the lines offers a chance to look at some writing-related issues:

- practising using a **capital letter** for the personal **pronoun** *I*
- writing sentences featuring **subordination** (*When ...*), with the contrasting **conjunction** (*But ...*) in the final line
- writing consistently in the **past tense** for six lines and then the sudden shift to the **present tense** in line 7
- adding the **comma** before the main clause.

✱ Which of these elements you choose to focus on will inevitably depend on the needs of individual writers.

Note: If possible, add a selection of photos of the children at various ages to your display of their poems.

Welcome to Word World!

> 90g box of awesome adverbs £3.50
> 2L bottle of super suffixes £1.00
> 50cl tub of quick question marks £1.99
> 1.13kg carton of lively letters 75p
> 295g packet of curly commas £1.50
> 2kg bag of fantastic full stops £2.75
>
> Extract from a group-made piece

What to do

* Key Stage 1 classrooms teem with language – and rightly so. The notion here is that you have so much language and you know so much about it that you should open a supermarket, selling bits of language to those who need more and aren't the experts that you are.

* Across the whole of Key Stage 1, the curriculum for English specifies well over 20 items of linguistic terminology that children should have explicit knowledge of. This gives you plenty of material for the shelves! Of course, you can tackle this activity first of all by only including items you feel your children should know and then adding to it as their experience and understanding grows.

* Once you have explained the idea of *Word World* to the children, it's helpful to ask them to bring into class items of food packaging, so you can explore together how everyday foodstuffs are measured and priced.

* Talk together about the language terms they know and maybe display these for all to see and draw on in their writing.

* Explain that each term for sale needs a quantity and a price – and crucially an **adjective** to make the item attractive to customers. If the adjective can **alliterate** with the item, even better.

Differentiation suggestion

* As a development, individual terms might be expanded into large posters for display and include actual examples of each item – for example, a lemonade bottle with exclamation marks bursting out the top, or a cereal packet pouring out verbs.

Crazy Creatures

My Famous Frog

My frog eats sprouts and leftover candyfloss.
    It is as smooth as a cushion.
My frog drinks dark red fizzy cranberry juice.
    It is as colourful as a swimming pool.
My frog can jump over the moon.
    It is as fantastic as a cow playing cards.

                      Michael

Crazy Creatures

What to do

*   Michael knows perfectly well that there is no frog in the world quite like the one he describes in his poem on page 144. But, because he knows a few things about real frogs, he's able to revel in his ability to imagine some fantastically impossible alternatives.

*   Ask the children to imagine they are explorers; they travel the world looking for brand-new, never-before-seen animals. Now, in their writing, they are going to tell the world about their latest amazing discovery.

*   Each sentence of their writing will tell their readers one more thing about what the animal does: what it eats, what it drinks, where it lives, how it moves, what it can do, and so on. And each detail must be as crazily inventive as they can make it.

*   A second sequence of lines describes what the animal is like. Writers need to keep their writing fresh and varied, and therefore as engaging as the animal itself. So now the sentences will begin, not by naming the animal, but with the **pronoun** *It*.

*   Each of these lines will also be built round a **simile**: *as ... as*. Here, ask writers to say what the animal looks like, what it is like to the touch, its colours, its shape, its brain, and so on. And to keep the overall tone of the writing, children should again be encouraged to be extravagant.

*   In his six lines, Michael alternated the two elements and styles of the piece. Your writers can do the same or present each collection of lines as two separate verses.

*   Finally, add an inviting title: an alliterating adjective to fit the animal usually does the trick.

All Things Bright and Beautiful

Buttercups yellow as egg yolk.
Daisies white like fresh snow.
Bluebells as blue as summer.
Poppies as red as ketchup.
Sunflowers gold as pirates' treasure.

Avia

All Things Bright and Beautiful

What to do

* This activity attempts to create a small garden in words – a garden full of colour and also a very neat and tidy one.

* As you can see in Avia's poem on page 146, each line starts with a different flower. The line is then developed into an **expanded noun phrase** built around a single **simile** in which the flower is compared to something else of the same colour.

* Avia's poem has five flowers – and each line has just five words. This keeps the writing clear and crisp.

* Begin by making a class collection of flowers. Here are some to add to the ones in Avia's poem:

    dandelion   rose   snowdrop   daffodil   pansy   tulip   heather   lily

* From the collection choose five and list them down your board. Introduce the idea of **similes** and how they work to make comparisons. Show how a simile can be written using one word: … like … or … as … ; or two words: … as … as …. This brings variety to the writing – and is invaluable for the word-count of each line.

* Complete the whole-group poem, using each of the three simile variants at least once and with comparisons that bring life to the lines.

* When children go on to create their own flower gardens, they will need to know that crossings out are quite okay! Writing can be messy just like painting and real gardening. These are deliberately short poems with their own rules; final, neat copies will not take long to make.

Differentiation suggestion

* More adventurous writers can feature six or seven flowers and therefore six or seven lines of six or seven words in each one.

To Boldly Go

Welcome to Aclimeha.

Bananas are blue and the sky is green.

The moon is a triangle.

Birds swim in the sea and fish live on clouds.

The queen is Rosa Parks.

A week has 10 days and a year has 13 months.

All the mummies and daddies go to school.

On Aclimeha 2 + 2 = 5.

Michaela

To Boldly Go

What to do

∗ It was Dr. Seuss who said, 'I like nonsense, it wakes up the brain cells'. That is exactly the spirit of this activity. Children relish silliness because it allows them to show that, in reality, they do understand things. Being asked to think nonsensically freshens up and exercises their thinking in a creative session of brain-gym.

∗ Begin by explaining to your writers that they are all astronomers and they have discovered a new planet. Because of their discovery, the planet's name will be made out of the letters of their own first name.

∗ The first task they have, therefore, is to write their first names, cut up the letters, and rearrange them to make the planet's name. Thus, they are making **anagrams**.

∗ The first line of their description of this planet can be, like Michaela's poem on page 148 'Welcome to' plus the anagram – with its **capital letter** to show that it is a name.

∗ The rest of their writing lets writers show off what they know by creating features of their planet, on which things are different/opposite to or just plain 'wrong' in relation to life here on earth.

∗ Encourage children to think right across the school curriculum, drawing on the range of their learning. This makes them consider a breadth of material to draw on for ideas and gives the overall descriptions their necessary (and entertaining) variety.

∗ Some children will write just one idea in each line. However, if more confident writers want to include two bits of nonsense for any single subject, then, like Michaela, they can do this by creating **compound sentences** using *and*.

∗ For a last line, writers can, as in Michaela's example, repeat the planet's name with one final, brain-cell-waking detail.

The Incredible It

The Incredible It

It is as big as a castle in a forest and as tiny as a crumb falling from a biscuit.

It is as red as a curtain to the puppet show and as blue as the sea for a pirate ship to sail on.

It is as noisy as all a school laughing in assembly and as speechless as when you're fast asleep in bed.

It is as jazzy as a clown's clothes and as invisible as a ghost walking down the school corridor.

It lives in a land far away and in my grandad's garden shed.

Elliot

The Incredible It

What to do

✳ Basically, this is quite a simple activity, but as Elliot shows, one with lots of potential for some sophisticated writing and vocabulary.

✳ The idea is to create in words a fantastically impossible creature – *The Incredible It*. Each sentence of the description of the *It* includes three key features:

1. Each sentence is a **compound**, using the **conjunction** *and*
2. Each half of the compound includes the **simile** *'as … as'*
3. The two similes feature adjectives with different or opposite meanings – **antonyms**.

✳ Start by writing up the title and ask the children if they can offer other words that are the same or similar in meaning to *Incredible* (synonyms) – *'Amazing'*, *'Great'*, perhaps. List their offerings below the original adjective and ask them to write their own title, *The … It*, with any one of the synonyms in the middle. This at once introduces one of the features of the writing that is to come.

✳ The repeated pattern of each sentence is *It is as … as … and as … as …*

✳ For each sentence, the children now write down its beginning and then are given or choose a pair of antonyms. Here are some you might offer:

hot / cold	big / small	old / new	loud / quiet
fast / slow	friendly / unfriendly	weak / strong	hard / soft

✳ As with the title, ask the writers for synonyms for each adjective in the pair to allow for choice and variety in the writing. Repeat the process for the second half of the sentence.

✳ Encourage writers to add interesting details to their ideas each time, though there will be times when one word is strong enough.

✳ For his closing line, Elliot was asked to write where his It lives, and in the spirit of the piece it had to be two very different places. You might try the same idea.

Note: in the current curriculum, children aren't expected to meet the terms **synonym** and **antonym** until Year 6. However, Key Stage 1 children are well able to grasp and use the concepts even if the explicit terminology isn't used at this stage.

The Magic of Metaphors

My bed is a purple steam locomotive and on it I travel to the countryside.

It is a cheetah chasing antelope in the valley.

My bed is a Tony the Tiger hot air balloon and it flies over an amusement park.

It is Catbells with animals eating grass on it.

It is Apollo 11 to fly to the moon with me every night.

Matthew

The Magic of Metaphors

What to do

✱ The obvious difference between a **simile** and a **metaphor** is that one uses '*like*' and one doesn't. However, the real difference is that while a simile says something just resembles something else, a metaphor says something is something else. Metaphors are transformers and, therefore, magical.

✱ In his poem on page 152, Matthew uses the magic of metaphors to say in each line that his bed is something different, something new, something exciting.

✱ To introduce the power of metaphors, read Matthew's poem with the children and explore the idea of turning one thing into something else. Focus on the everyday ordinariness of our beds, which therefore makes the changes all the more dramatic.

✱ Use a line-by-line approach with the writers and invite them to imagine their beds as something different in every line.

✱ Here are some ideas for transformations:

   ✦ If your bed becomes a vehicle, something to travel in, what will it be?

   ✦ If your bed turns into a wild animal, what will it be?

   ✦ If your bed changes into the weather, what will it become?

   ✦ If your bed turns into a food or drink, what will it be?

   ✦ If your bed becomes a building, what will it be?

✱ Remind the children – with every line, if necessary – that it is the details a writer adds to each transformation that will bring the metaphor fully to life.

✱ To create variety, ask writers to start lines both *My bed is …* and *It is …*, possibly on alternate lines.

✱ The poet Sylvia Plath died in 1963. In 1976 Faber published *The Bed Book*, poems originally written for Plath's own children. It is pure delight and a perfect introduction to beds-as-metaphors. You can find the full text – with illustrations by Quentin Blake (among others) – online and there are readings of the poems on YouTube.

Digging Into Dictionaries

A careful cat is catching carpets calmly.

A doting dolphin is dodging doors dottily.

A pink pig is pinching pies playfully.

Martine and Danielle

Digging Into Dictionaries

What to do

* The curriculum for English requires that Year 2 children are taught and understand the terms **noun**, **adjective**, **verb** and **adverb**. To aid their understanding and their practice, this activity is intended to aid children's understanding for these terms and get them exploring the treasure-house that is a dictionary.

* The children need a dictionary that offers a good range of vocabulary and specifies the word class for each item. They will also need a sheet of paper with columns and lines like this:

1	2 (adjective)	3 (singular-noun)	4	5 (verb)	6 (plural noun)	7 (adverb)
A			is			
A			is			
A			is			

* The girls' lines on page 154 incorporate all four of the prescribed word classes, but you can adapt the method for your less able writers by giving them a reduced grid, focussing on the elements you think most useful to them.

* For the full activity, start by asking children to choose an animal and write it in column 3. They should know this word is a **noun**.

* Next, have them look this animal up in their dictionary. If their animal is included, fine; if not, they should simply find the place where their animal should be alphabetically.

* Now, they use their dictionary to go on a word-hunt. You might need to show children how dictionary entries are presented, and word classes identified.

* Ask them what their animal is like and explain that, in their dictionaries, they need to find an **adjective** for column 2, starting with the same letter as the animal. They are now ready to make their own tongue-twisting sentences, like the examples on page 154.

* Next comes the **verb** in column 5 – in its **present progressive** form; so is + verb + *ing*;

* Then, another **noun**, in column 6 which needs to be made **plural**.

* Finally, the second **adjective**, in column 7, made into an **adverb** by adding the suffix *-ly*, all starting with the same letter as that initial animal!

* Encourage a high degree of silliness in the sentences and be sure to see whose twisters twist tongues the most. Children can write final drafts on plain paper without the columns.

Acknowledgements

We are grateful to the following for permission to reproduce copyright material:

The poem "Now We Are Six" / "The End" from Now We Are Six by A. A. Milne, copyright © The Pooh Properties Trust 1927; copyright © Penguin Random House LLC, 1927. Copyright © renewed by A. A. Milne, 1955. Reproduced with permissions from Curtis Brown Group Ltd on behalf of The Pooh Properties Trust; and Dutton Children's Books, an imprint of Penguin Young Readers Group, a division of Penguin Random House LLC. All rights reserved; The poem "Cottage" by Eleanor Farjeon, published in Then There were Three, Michael Joseph, copyright © Miss E Farjeon Will Trust. Reproduced by permission of David Higham Associates; and the poem "Quietly" by Aenaone Tickler. Reproduced with kind permission of the author.

References

The poem 'Moods and Tenses' on page 7 can be found in *I Saw Esau – The Schoolchild's Pocket Book*, edited by Iona and Peter Opie, published by Walker Books in 1992.

An extract from Henry Wadsworth Longfellow's poem 'Rain in Summer' is used on page 15. The full version can be found here: https://www.hwlongfellow.org/poems_poem.php?pid=84.

The activity on page 45 is inspired by the tile of John Burningham's book, *Would you Rather ...*, first published by Jonathan Cape in 1978, and subsequently by Red Fox in 1999.

The inspiration for the activity on page 61 is an old comic song called 'We're off in a Motor Car'. You can find lots of performances of it on YouTube.

The starting point for the activity on pages 66-67 is Mary Ann Hoberman's poem 'Giraffes', first published by Little, Brown.

An idea in Kenneth Koch's book, *Wishes, Lies and Dreams*, first published by Chelsea House Publishers in 1970, was the starting point for the activity on page 69.

The poem 'You Are Old, Father William' on page 85 can be found in Chapter 5 of Lewis Carroll's *Alice's Adventures in Wonderland*.

The Christina Rossetti poem, 'What are Heavy?' on page 93 first appeared in her collection for children entitled *Sing-Song*, published by Macmillan in 1893.

The activity on page 97 uses Christina Rossetti's poem, 'What is Pink?' as its starting point.

The activity on page 101 makes reference to *The BFG* by Roald Dahl, originally published by Jonathan Cape in 1982, and subsequently by Penguin Books.

This activity on page 104 was inspired by a collection of animals' pleas in *Prayers from the Ark and the Creatures' Choir* by Carmen Bernos de Gasztold, translated from the French by Rumer Godden, published by Penguin Books in 1976. Examples of the poems are readily available online.

The poem 'Three were three ghostesses' on page 125 can be found in *I Saw Esau – The Schoolchild's Pocket Book*, edited by Iona and Peter Opie, published by Walker Books in 1992.

Sylvia Plath's poem 'The Magic of Metaphors' was the inspiration for the activity on pages 152-53. The poem appears in *The Bed Book*, published by Faber in 1970.. The complete poem with illustrations by Quentin Blake can be found at www.brainpickings.org.